Also by Carol Berkin

———

A Brilliant Solution: Inventing the American Constitution

First Generations: Women in Colonial America

Civil War Wives: The Lives and Times of Angelina Grimke Weld, Varina Howell Davis & Julia Dent Grant

Revolutionary Mothers: Women in the Struggle for America's Independence

Wondrous Beauty: The Life and Adventures of Elizabeth Patterson Bonaparte

The Bill of Rights

The Fight to Secure America's Liberties

CAROL BERKIN

Simon & Schuster

New York   London   Toronto   Sydney   New Delhi

Simon & Schuster
1230 Avenue of the Americas
New York, NY 10020

First Simon & Schuster hardcover edition May 2015

SIMON & SCHUSTER and colophon are registered trademarks of Simon & Schuster, Inc.

For information about special discounts for bulk purchases, please contact Simon & Schuster Special Sales at 1-866-506-1949 or business@simonandschuster.com.

The Simon & Schuster Speakers Bureau can bring authors to your live event. For more information or to book an event contact the Simon & Schuster Speakers Bureau at 1-866-248-3049 or visit our website at www.simonspeakers.com.

Interior design by Robert E. Ettlin

Manufactured in the United States of America

1   3   5   7   9   10   8   6   4   2

Library of Congress Cataloging-in-Publication Data

Berkin, Carol.
The Bill of Rights : the fight to secure America's liberties / Carol Berkin.
    pages cm
    1. United States. Constitution. 1st–10th Amendments. 2. Civil rights—United States—History. 3. Constitutional history—United States. 4. Madison, James, 1751–1836. I. Title.
    KF4749.B45 2015
    342.7303'9—dc23

2014012843

ISBN 978-1-4767-4379-0
ISBN 978-1-4767-4381-3 (ebook)

To my granddaughter, Talulla Thomas Joyce

Contents

Contents

The Bill of Rights

Prologue

———

For the majority of modern Americans, the Bill of Rights stands as the most important element of the Constitution, the touchstone, as James Madison hoped it would become, of our shared unalienable rights and liberties. Along with the Declaration of Independence, these first ten amendments—with their guarantees of freedom of speech, religion, and the press, and the right to assemble; their promise of a speedy trial by jury; their protection against double jeopardy and unreasonable search and seizure; and their recognition of the right to bear arms—announce to the world our national values and ideals. They have served as the standards by which we measure our individual actions and the actions of our government toward its own citizens.

Yet hallowed by time as the Declaration and the Bill of Rights have become, it is crucial to place these two documents in their historical context and examine the immediate circumstances that generated them. The men who created the Declaration did so to justify a revolution, and the men who passed the Bill of Rights acted to secure the loyalty of citizens wary of their new federal government.

The men who debated, revised, and campaigned for and against the first ten amendments were eighteenth-century Americans. Their world is not ours. The memories they carried were of imperial abuses, the painful renunciation of their English identities, and a long and exhausting war for independence. The excitement they felt and the fears that haunted them were the result of a rare opportunity to create a new nation and to establish it as a republic. If they knew they were making history, they did not know what that history would be.

The men who produced the Bill of Rights were neither demigods nor visionaries. They were mere mortals, some brilliant, some quite ordinary, most of them wealthier and better educated than their neighbors. Almost all of them were veteran politicians, and though most of the issues they grappled with will seem foreign to us today, the tempo and tone of their politics will be familiar. In their wrangling and debating, in their manipulation of procedure to expedite their agenda or derail that of their opponents, in the flare-ups of ego and the indulgence of idiosyncrasy, and in the combustible mixture of self-interest, ideals, and principles that propelled them, these men resemble political leaders of every era. But in their burden of serving in a government without precedents and with uncertain legitimacy, in their pressing anxiety that this government might fail, and in their knowledge that America was dwarfed by the great imperial powers across the Atlantic, they are uniquely men of the late eighteenth century.

In 1789, when James Madison proposed the Bill of Rights, the young nation faced a great ideological divide with regard to a question that is being revived today: should broad power and authority reside in the federal government, as the Federalists wished, or should it reside in the state governments, where the Antifederalists insisted it could best protect the people's liberties? In these early years of the new nation, this ideological struggle was raw and fraught with immediacy, for the Constitution that empowered the national government was new and lacked the traditions that over time lend legitimacy and elicit loyalty. The political decisions the men of this early era made forestalled but did not dissolve the tension between localism and nationalism that was endemic to the federal system they created. That tension would reemerge in the nineteenth century when challenges to federal law and policy led to the Civil War. Even in our lifetime, this issue of where ultimate power should reside remains a Gordian knot.

This confrontation between states' rights and national authority started with the fierce debates over ratification of the Constitution, and it continued in the First Federal Congress, in the state legislatures, and in the press as Washington's first administration began. We can appreciate the Bill of Rights only in the context of this struggle. These amendments, conceived by James Madison, one of the most astute Federalists of his day, were intended to weaken, if not crush, the continuing opposition to the new federal government he had been so instrumental in creating. By assuring citizens that the new government would honor and protect their liberties, he hoped to achieve two interlocking goals. The first was to ease the fear of tyranny harbored by many within the general populace and thus separate the Antifederalist followers from their leaders. The second was to preempt the Antifederalists' plans to pass amendments that would severely restrict the powers of the new government.

Madison's Bill of Rights was thus more a political strategy than a statement of America's most cherished values. Yet Madison was keenly aware of its potential to set a high standard for the relationship between citizens and the men who governed them. Even more important to Madison, this explicit guarantee of rights and liberties could play a critical role in protecting minority groups from abuse by the majority. The addition of these amendments was thus a patriotic as well as a political measure, for it was designed to strengthen republican values and to ensure that the American government would honor the people's right to life, liberty, and the pursuit of happiness. It was the genius of James Madison that he could unite practical considerations and noble aspirations, and join the ideological with the ideal.

All of the rights Madison wished to protect had their roots in the founding generation's colonial and revolutionary past. They speak to imperial abuses and to hallowed Anglo-American traditions that do not resonate today. Yet the generations that followed added their understandings of these rights just as today we add our own. In this way, the amendments once dismissed as only a "parchment barrier" remains our collective heritage and we remain its guardian for future generations.

I

On September 12, 1787, Virginian George Mason rose on the floor of what came to be known as the constitutional convention.[1] He proposed that the delegates gathered in Independence Hall add a bill of rights to the Constitution they had just created. The response Mason received was a resounding no. Was it possible that the men we call the founding fathers opposed such basic rights as freedom of speech, the press, or conscience? Was their intention to introduce a new tyranny to replace the tyranny of George III and his government? Why was Mason's request so firmly denied?

The answer is simple. These men were weary on that fateful September day. They had been meeting since mid-May, trudging through the rain on many a morning or wiping the perspiration from their brows on those days when the stifling heat and humidity of an all too typical Philadelphia summer seemed unbearable. Their evenings had been spent in the cramped quarters above the city's many taverns, in rooms occupied by two and sometimes three men. Most surely slept fitfully, sharing beds in rooms redolent of spittoons and chamber pots, the smells intensified by the need to keep the shutters tightly closed against a summer invasion of bluebottled flies. Far from home, countinghouse, law office, plantation, or farm, they fretted about inventories, clients, and crops, with no choice but to rely on the good sense of family members or employees to ensure that their fortunes did not suffer. As the weeks dragged by, they longed for the comforts of home, the satisfactions of a well-cooked meal, and the companionship of wives and children. Yet they stayed.

They stayed because the business they had come to Philadelphia to do was too important to abandon. They were there, they believed, to save their country. They feared that their experiment in republican government was in danger of invasion or, worse, of internal collapse if a new government was not created to replace the "league of friendship" known as the Confederation, which had proved woefully inadequate to deal with the problems facing America.

The Articles of Confederation, America's first constitution, did not owe its creation to a lapse of judgment on the part of the Revolutionary generation. To the men who wrote it, this very restricted government seemed to perfectly embody the goals of their Revolution. They did not yet think of themselves as citizens of a unified nation; like their neighbors, they thought of themselves as Marylanders, Virginians, New Yorkers, or Connecticut men. Their history and their historical circumstances made this a reasonable identification. Their newly independent states had once been colonies—colonies with different patterns of settlement, different mixes of ethnic and religious populations, and different internal histories. Virginia did not share New York's Dutch origins; Connecticut's lingering Puritan heritage was alien to Pennsylvania's Quaker roots. And Maryland's religious wars between Catholics and Protestants had no parallel in Georgia or North Carolina. It was true that by the time the war for independence began, all the rebellious colonies did have some striking political similarities. In each, the local legislature was elected by men whose race and property ownership qualified them to full citizenship. But families who traced their history back to Barbados refugees in South Carolina did not feel a natural affinity for the men and women who fled religious persecution to settle Massachusetts. Thus it was not surprising that, when asked what his *country* was, a leading revolutionary like Patrick Henry could immediately respond, "Virginia is my country, sir." In short, the men who represented their rebellious states in the Continental Congress—and later in the Confederation Congress—were loyal not to something so vague as the United States but to their own state.

Travel and communication in the eighteenth century reinforced this loyalty to place that we today might dismiss as provincialism. The great revolutions in transportation and communication lay decades ahead in the nineteenth century. In 1776, when the Articles of Confederation were written, horses and horse-drawn carriages, often moving along little more than Indian paths, were the fastest modes of transportation. Travel from Boston to the Continental Congress in Philadelphia could take weeks if roads were washed out by rain or if rivers had risen too high for a man on horseback to ford. Indeed, to many a Georgian in the late eighteenth century, a trip to Massachusetts might as well have been a voyage to the moon. Ships, it was true, could sail along the coast of these mainland states, but few Georgia farmers were likely to be on board.

Communication was unpredictable and cumbersome. Letters often found their way to their intended recipients through elaborate relays: entrusted first to friends heading to port cities, then passed on to ship captains heading in the right direction, and finally turned over to local residents who promised to deliver them to the addressee. Much depended on whether any link in this chain failed; and even when the system worked, it could take months for a letter to find its way from writer to reader. News traveled just as slowly in a world where not every household had access to a daily newspaper. Often the best source of news was travelers, especially ship captains, who brought with them newspapers already several months old.

Under these circumstances, provincialism or localism was reasonable, even among men more privileged, better traveled, and more sophisticated than their neighbors. But ideology, as much as circumstances, played a critical role in the belief that a "league of friendship" among thirteen separate and sovereign nation-states fulfilled the goals of the Revolution.

The men who fought for independence had rallied to the cry "No taxation without representation." And to them, this meant no taxation by any legislature other than their local assembly. The Lockean contract—that a legitimate government must represent the interests and protect the liberties of those it governed—had been reinterpreted by free Americans; it meant that only a government composed of men you knew, men who lived among you and shared your interests, deserved your obedience, your loyalty—and your taxes. As they began a war for independence against a distant government, made up of men who would not suffer the consequences of the taxes they imposed, Americans believed the only safeguard against such tyranny was to put power in the hands of local legislatures.

Thus the Continental Congress produced a constitution that preserved the sovereignty of the states and restricted the powers of the national government to the barest essentials: to coordinate the military and diplomatic war effort against Great Britain.[2] Even this was miraculous, because the colonies had never before cooperated. But, as they prepared to wage a war against the most powerful army and navy in the world, American leaders recognized the need for unity.

The constitution they drafted was, in many ways, a defense against a new tyranny. Their enemy had taxed them from afar, and had regulated their trade and commerce; they would avoid creating another government with such powers. They would avoid suffering under a new tyrant by refusing to create a separate executive branch. They would deprive the government of the power to tax or dictate trade policy. They would not allow it to introduce a uniform currency that could prevent each state from providing its own citizens with ready cash. Above all, they would avoid attempts by large states to dominate small ones by ensuring a rule of one state, one vote in the new government.

The Articles of Confederation embodied the hopes and fears of the revolutionaries. They were a culmination of the colonies' 150 years of history as possessions of a powerful empire. But in the effort to avoid the oppressions of the past, the men who wrote this constitution did not provide for the problems of the future.[3]

Those problems had emerged even before the ink on the peace treaty was dry in 1783. Peace brought a lingering postwar economic depression, as America adjusted to its independence from Great Britain's protective, though often smothering, embrace. No longer escorted by Royal Navy vessels, American merchant ships carrying cargoes meant for Mediterranean buyers became easy targets for North African pirates. In New England, shippers discovered how much they had depended on trade with the Caribbean islands that flew the British flag. In Georgia and South Carolina, states that had suffered the devastation of two major British campaigns during the war, planters found themselves scrambling to find new slaves to replace those who had fled to the welcoming arms of the British army.

The new nation faced the embarrassment of debts to European allies that it could not pay. The government, forced to rely on requisitions from the states, found itself helpless to establish its credit, and efforts to borrow more money from Holland and France were futile. To the great embarrassment of the members of the Confederation Congress, the government was also unable to pay military veterans or repay the civilians who had sacrificed crops and livestock to the war effort. Confidence in the government's ability to honor the promissory notes, called "continentals," that it had given to farmers, merchants, and artisans could be measured by the popular term for worthlessness—"not worth a continental."

Four years after the war ended, the new nation's borders stood virtually undefended against Indians or European powers. Britain still occupied its forts in the Ohio Valley, and alliances forming among displaced or threatened Indian tribes boded ill for eager American settlers.

Perhaps most troubling of all was that the spirit of cooperation, which had reigned among the states during the struggle for independence, had evaporated. Thirteen separate nation-states now vied with one another for advantages in commerce and trade. Each established trade barriers at its borders and thus duties had to be paid at every state line. Price gouging by New York, whose port city brought in vital foreign goods, enriched New Yorkers and enraged consumers in New Jersey and Connecticut. To the south, Virginia shamelessly exploited the consumer needs of North Carolina. Every state had its own currency, and some of this was worthless paper. Small wonder that interstate trade was in chaos, making recovery from postwar depression even more difficult.

By the time the Philadelphia convention met, the members of the Confederation Congress, sitting in New York City, had thrown up their hands and surrendered any hope of solving these pressing problems. Surveying the situation, the former commander in chief of the Continental Army, George Washington, lamented that the Confederation was a mere shadow of a government. And William Pierce of Georgia described the Confederation as "a ship bearing under the weight of a tempest; it is trembling, and just on the point of sinking."[4]

The men who met in Philadelphia agreed with these sentiments. Clearly, something had to be done to save their country. And this was why, by September 1787, the delegates to the convention had put themselves through over four grueling months of debate, discussion, and often heated argument. This is why they endured cramped quarters, dismal weather, and a steady diet of tavern food. Behind locked doors and draped windows, they had undertaken the task of writing a new constitution.

If any group was up to the challenge, these fifty-four delegates were. Gathered in Independence Hall were members of America's economic and social elite, men far better educated and more widely traveled than their farmer and shopkeeper neighbors. And, in a society that still assumed men of wealth should hold the reins of government, their political leadership experience was broad and deep. They had learned politics at the dinner table, listening to fathers, uncles, cousins, and older brothers. They had studied rhetoric and political philosophy at colleges at home and abroad and most of them were trained in the law. They had served in Continental Congresses, colonial assemblies, and state legislatures. They had overseen trials as justices of the peace and directed state policies as governors. During the Revolution, many had led men into battle as Continental Army officers, and thus they had observed firsthand how that experience had unified men of every region and state. Many, though not all of them, had been born or educated abroad and this background, like their army experience, had given them a less provincial perspective than most of their fellow members of the American elite. They were, in Alexander Hamilton's apt phrase, men who "thought continentally," men who wanted to create a nation, not a loosely knit confederation of squabbling states.

The charge they had been given by the Confederation Congress was narrow: propose amendments to strengthen the current constitution. But men like Virginia's James Madison, New York's Alexander Hamilton, Pennsylvania's Benjamin Franklin, and the universally admired George Washington believed the crisis was too serious for mere patchwork. Thus, within the first week of the convention, the delegates had agreed to abandon what they saw as a faulty government and create a new one.

The men who made this decision to abandon one frame of government and create another understood the challenge they faced—and they were uncertain if they were wise enough to meet it. But they knew they had models to guide them. Behind them were two centuries of Anglo-American political culture, with its emphasis on the rule of law, its limitations on the power of the men in office, and its threefold division of government into executive, legislative, and judicial branches. Their republic would have no king and no legislative branch belonging to the aristocracy, of course—this was one legacy of their Revolution. But whatever form the new framework took, it would draw its authority from the consent of the governed.

Many of the delegates had participated in the arduous process of drafting and seeing ratified their state constitutions. But they knew that the superimposition of what eighteenth-century men called an "energetic" national government on thirteen quarrelsome mini nations, each jealously guarding its sovereignty, would be far more controversial. This is why anxiety, thick as the summer humidity, hung over the convention throughout its months of deliberation.

The delegates knew that the government they designed must have far more power than the one they sought to replace. The question was: how much power? Ardent nationalists like Madison, Hamilton, and Pennsylvania's brilliant, flamboyant Gouverneur Morris wanted to provide a full panoply of powers: the right to tax, to regulate foreign and interstate trade, to raise an army for defense, and to establish a uniform currency. Above all, they wished to create a truly national government able to win the loyalty of citizens of every state. But this was far from a goal shared outside the convention walls. Many of the political leaders who refused to attend this convention did not wish to see such a transfer of loyalty. Devoted revolutionaries like Samuel Adams of Massachusetts and Patrick Henry of Virginia continued to believe that representative government meant local government. When Henry learned of the gathering in Philadelphia, his judgment was succinct: "I smell a rat," he declared, for he was certain the delegates intended to abandon the Articles and propose a new government. Men like Henry were immune to Hamilton's plea that Americans think continentally. They embraced the political certainty that only a local government could understand and serve the interests of the citizens.

Even within the convention, Madison and Hamilton knew, there were delegates wary of creating a government that would erode the autonomy of the states. The divided loyalties of the former governor of Virginia, thirty-four-year-old Edmund Randolph; the cranky but clever Elbridge Gerry of Massachusetts; and many of the men from smaller states would be revealed in the daily efforts to thread the needle between the preservation of state authority and the empowering of a central government.

Compromise was the watchword of the convention's deliberation, but perseverance proved the mode. Debates and arguments over the structure and shape of the new national government were long and often redundant. Over the months, the convention repeatedly circled back to revive issues once deemed resolved. No vote ever seemed final, no decision above reconsideration. What could not be resolved was sent to committees, where debate continued but the pressure to compromise was greater.

Although the convention adjourned each day around 4 p.m., discussion often continued long into the night. Caucuses of like-minded state delegations met to plan the next day's strategy, while anxious men gathered to tally and re-tally potential votes. On the best of evenings, essential compromises were hammered out over a glass or two of good port wine.

By July, the general shape of the new government and the scope of its powers had been decided. While these powers would seem broad to many opponents of the Constitution, they may seem curiously limited to modern sensibilities. To the founders, the national government's raison d'être was threefold: the defense of the country's borders, the maintenance of law and order at home, and the establishment of a stable and expanding economy based on good credit. These powers were, in effect, to be siphoned away from the states in an arrangement that was truly novel for the eighteenth-century world: it was called *federalism*. Under this system of shared sovereignty, the national government acquired some exclusive powers, the states retained exclusive rights to others, and some belonged to both.

Under federalism, the convention left untouched and unchallenged many of the powers enjoyed by the state governments. States would determine voting requirements, they would determine the fate of slavery within their borders, they retained taxing powers, and they maintained their own judicial systems. The delegates were practical politicians, not idealists, and they understood the limit of their capacity to wrest power from the states where it resided.

Some delegates believed the states would reject federalism. A few delegates would, in the end, refuse to sign a document that they felt robbed the states of too much autonomy. On the other hand, the devout nationalist Alexander Hamilton felt that federalism left the task of nation-building incomplete. His solution struck most of the delegates as even more extreme and surely less realistic: Hamilton proposed to abolish the states.

Weeks and months of argument, debate, and compromise took their toll. Patience had grown short as August turned to September and nerves were frazzled. By September 12, the delegates believed that all that stood between them and home were a few small, finishing touches to their new Constitution. And then, George Mason demanded a statement of the rights and liberties of the people.

Mason's proposal on that fateful September day took the majority of delegates by surprise. Only the men of the Committee on Detail, charged with polishing the language of the Constitution, might have seen it coming, for South Carolina's brash young delegate, Charles Pinckney, had pressed them in late August to add a guarantee of several rights to the document. The committee had rejected the idea. Now Mason had revived it, calling on the whole convention to produce a national bill of rights.

No one doubted Mason's sincerity, for his reputation as a champion of rights was well known at the convention. A scion of a wealthy planter family, the sixty-two-year-old Mason had authored his own state's Declaration of Rights, making Virginia the first state to guarantee freedom of the press, tolerance of religion, protection from unreasonable searches, and the right to a fair and speedy trial. What the delegates did doubt, however, was Mason's sanguine assurances that the drafting of a bill of rights could be done quickly. They knew from experience that nothing at the convention was speedily done. A nightmare vision arose of days of wrangling and debate. What rights would they agree to include? How could they be certain these were the most deserving of protection? If a critical right was overlooked, would that mean it was denied to the people? Did the inclusion of some rights mean, inevitably, the exclusion of others? Was there unanimity to be found on the definition of any right? If not, its simple phrasing could take hours of discussion—or, worse, added committee work.

Heated opposition to Mason's proposal emerged quickly. Pennsylvania's Gouverneur Morris resisted any further tampering with the convention's handiwork. No doubt Morris's role in editing and refining the language of the final draft contributed to his adamant refusal to tolerate any last-minute changes or additions. But it was Connecticut's Roger Sherman, the cobbler turned lawyer, whose stern demeanor and terse speech conveyed a rectitude that many admired, who best expressed the general feelings of the convention: Mason's concern was groundless. The people's rights, Sherman said, clearly remained under the protection of the states, eight of which had included a bill of rights in their constitutions. The convention had given the national government no jurisdiction in the matter of the people's rights and liberties. It could not restrict them; it could not expand them; it could not endanger them. There was, in short, no need to protect Americans against powers the proposed government did not have.[5]

And there, to the relief of almost everyone, the matter ended. Or so it seemed. Yet, even before the struggles over ratification of the new Constitution began in the states, some astute delegates realized they had made a serious tactical error. In refusing to add a bill of rights, the men who supported the Constitution had handed their opponents the most powerful weapon in their arsenal.

II

If the convention was over, a fierce struggle to win ratification of its work was just beginning. Perhaps the intensity of this ratification battle arose from the unspoken similarities between supporters and opponents of the proposed Constitution rather than their vocal differences. Both embraced Locke's theory that government was a contract between sovereign people and the men they elected to govern them. It was this political paradigm that had justified the American Revolution and committed those who waged it to the creation of a republic rather than the establishment of a new monarchy. Men on both sides of the ratification issue had fought for independence, and had embraced this republican ideal. Yet this agreement raised a question: what form should their republic take and how extensive should its powers be? It was here that the arguments began.[1]

Most citizens agreed that the Articles of Confederation government was proving inadequate, but were they ready to accept a new Constitution? Would the costs of abandoning the Articles outweigh the benefits to American citizens? Should this new Constitution be adopted or should the Articles be amended just enough to ensure the safety of American borders and to encourage more cooperation among the states? The risk, as those who simply wanted to strengthen the Articles saw it, was that a strong national government could easily become a tyranny and the rights and liberties won in the Revolution would once again be challenged. The leading opponents of ratification were thus prepared to argue that the price to be paid for nationhood was too high.[2]

The men who led the constitutional convention had made their choice clear: they were nation-builders who wanted an energetic government strong enough to weld thirteen separate sovereignties into one. But they knew that in every state, influential men were preparing to rally opposition to ratification. The opposition's desire to defeat the Constitution was as intense as Madison's and Hamilton's desire to see it triumph. If these opponents could not defeat the proposed new government, they were determined to see it altered so that its powers were severely diminished. The alterations they wanted were not simply those that would better ensure the people's liberties; they were amendments that would restore the supremacy of the states. For these men, the two goals were the same, for in their view, the protection of rights and liberties would best be provided by local state governments.

Even before the states began to organize their ratifying conventions, the framers realized they had made a serious mistake in rejecting George Mason's demand for a bill of rights. Perhaps no one recognized this political error more fully than James Madison. He firmly believed a bill of rights was unnecessary in a government with carefully delineated and limited powers. Yet he was politically astute enough to see what an effective weapon the framers had put in the hands of the opposition. If these men wielded it well, they might achieve their goal: the defeat of the Constitution and the restoration of the autonomy and supremacy of state governments.

A heroic effort was needed to secure ratification, and James Madison was prepared to rise to the occasion. Yet no one looked less the part of a hero than the man whom friends and foes alike called little Jemmy Madison. Barely five feet four inches tall, Madison did not cut an imposing figure like his fellow Virginian, George Washington. Shy and socially awkward, he did not charm the ladies like the handsome, fair-haired Alexander Hamilton. He was neither cosmopolitan like the rakish Gouverneur Morris nor flamboyant and oratorically gifted like Patrick Henry. No one could imagine him moving effortlessly, as the radical organizer Samuel Adams did, between the drawing rooms of mansions and the crowded dockside taverns. Indeed, in his habitual black breeches, black silk stockings, and three-pointed black hat, with his powdered hair combed artlessly over his balding pate, Madison looked more like a Presbyterian minister than like one of Virginia's leading gentlemen politicians. Yet his unprepossessing physical appearance and demeanor belied a razor-sharp mind, a firm determination to defend his ideas, and a deep knowledge of politics both theoretical and practical. Massachusetts orator Fisher Ames might dismiss Madison as "a little too much of a book politician," but Georgia's delegate to the constitutional convention William Pierce declared the soft-spoken Mr. Madison "always the best informed man [on] any point in debate."[3]

Although he longed to return to his Virginia home, Montpelier, after the convention, Madison hurried instead to New York City, where the Confederation Congress was still sitting. He wanted to be in his seat when that Congress began to deliberate the fate of the Constitution and its own fate as well, for to send the Constitution to state ratifying conventions was to prepare the way for its own demise. Madison was well aware that the Confederation government was being asked to commit suicide.

Madison suspected that opponents of ratification would attempt to influence the Congress's response to the Constitution. His instincts proved correct. Richard Henry Lee, a member of one of the most influential families of Virginia and an avowed opponent of ratification, insisted that the Constitution was nothing more than a report from a convention. He suggested the Congress make any changes to the document the members saw fit. When this ploy to see the Constitution amended and its scope diminished by the sitting government did not work, Lee tried another tack. He proposed that congressmen who had been delegates to the Philadelphia convention should be barred from voting on accepting, rejecting, altering, or forwarding the Constitution.[4]

Both of Lee's maneuvers failed, perhaps because a dozen or more of the men who signed the Constitution sat in the Confederation Congress and were ready to defend it. In the end, the Congress chose to pass the Constitution along to state ratifying conventions without endorsement, rejection, or amendment. With that, the struggle shifted to the states, where propaganda began to flow in the newspapers, in letters, and in broadsides.

The nationalists staged the first coup in the ratification struggle by adopting the name Federalists and, more important, labeling their opponents Antifederalists. In truth, their opponents had an equal right to claim the designation "Federalists," for a majority of them preferred a *confederation* of sovereign states rather than an empowered national government. Instead, these "Antis" faced the disadvantage of waging the battle under a negative banner.

The Federalist forces were certainly impressive. Convention delegates such as George Washington, Alexander Hamilton, Roger Sherman, and Pennsylvania jurist James Wilson were joined by New York lawyer John Jay, and, from Massachusetts, Theodore Sedgwick and the eloquent Fisher Ames. Arrayed against them, however, were equally influential men: Virginia's George Mason, the acerbic but brilliant Elbridge Gerry of Massachusetts, Governor George Clinton of New York, and the famous revolutionary Samuel Adams of Massachusetts. In Hamilton's New York, the opposition was certain to be well organized by the sitting governor. And in Madison's and Washington's home state, Virginia, ratification faced some of its most formidable opponents, led by Patrick Henry, Richard Henry Lee, and the young Revolutionary War veteran James Monroe.

The propaganda on both sides was designed to influence the delegates to the state ratifying conventions. There was a spate of name-calling and mudslinging. Antis labeled Federalists as power-hungry, manipulative, and deceitful elitists who were openly dismissive of the people's rights. Federalists demeaned their opponents as "wicked," "malignant, ignorant and short-sighted triflers," "fools and knaves," and "a blind stupid set."[5]

The Antis were neither wicked nor ignorant, but some could be accused of self-interest. In New York, for example, Governor Clinton and his supporters were loath to turn over the regulation of trade, including the setting of domestic duties on imported goods, to a central government. Under the Articles, New York's merchants and shippers were free to reap impressive profits from the sale of goods entering through their port city to neighboring states. In southern states like South Carolina a heavy reliance on slave labor prompted many political leaders to cast wary eyes on a government that might, in the future, interfere with what would come to be called their "peculiar institution."[6]

The most widespread concerns, however, were ideological and philosophical. Many Antifederalists rejected the Federalists' claim that America was a country in crisis. Was America on the brink of internal collapse or conquest by more powerful nations? These men thought not. The country, they said, was not sunk in fatal economic depression. It was moving steadily toward widespread prosperity. Federalists might sound the alarm against the decline of patriotic virtues and the rise of selfishness and pettiness, but Antifederalists saw an optimistic country, its moral fiber strong and its citizens hardworking and content. During the Virginia ratifying convention, Patrick Henry would demand that all claims of crisis and impending disaster be put to the test. "I have thought, and still think," he declared "that a full investigation of the actual situation of America ought to precede any decision of this great and important question."[7]

Antifederalists were also troubled by the apparent ease with which the Philadelphia convention cast aside the Articles of Confederation. The delegates had been expected only to propose amendments to the Articles, yet they had secretly drafted a new Constitution. They had then compounded this reckless disregard for proper procedure by proposing ratifying conventions that bypassed both the Confederation Congress and the state legislatures. Such flagrant disregard for legality, Antifederalists feared, would breed new illegalities; under such circumstances, would any government be secure? As one Antifederalist warned, "the same reasons which you *now* urge for destroying our *present* federal government, may be urged for *abolishing the system* which you now propose." Here was a nightmare vision of endless political instability, of revolutions following revolutions, a vision of changes that would come so suddenly and so often that Americans would grow weary and embrace "any government, however despotic, that promises stability." [8]

To many Antifederalists, the readiness of the Philadelphia convention to overstep its instructions was a flagrant abuse of power. If delegates with explicit instructions could set them aside so easily, what assurances could be offered that the men sent to a national Congress would not be as quickly corrupted? The convention's imposition of secrecy was even more disturbing. From across the ocean in Paris, the American ambassador to France, Thomas Jefferson, voiced his profound disapproval at "the abominable precedent" of what he called "the tying up the tongues of the members." [9]

But the Antifederalists' most compelling argument was that the proposed Constitution was a betrayal of the principles and goals of the Revolution. The colonists, they said, had rebelled against oppression imposed from a distance by men who would not suffer the consequences of the laws they had passed, men who could not understand colonial America's needs—and men who simply did not care. Americans had fought their long war in order to create governments that would "be a true picture of the people," with legislators who "possess the knowledge of [the people's] circumstances and their wants; sympathize in all their distresses and be disposed to seek their true interests." Only sovereign state governments, the Antifederalists declared, fulfilled this revolutionary goal. [10]

The West Indian–born Alexander Hamilton, who had no deep roots in any state, might scorn these sentiments as mere provincialism. But to Antifederalists, provincialism was not a term of derogation; it was a badge of patriotism and honor. Reason and experience, not simply sentimental ties, made them wary of what they called "the consolidation of our Union." In a country as extensive as America, with such varied populations, economic interests, and religions, a league of friendship—no matter what its flaws— was best suited to the preservation of the people's liberty. The imposition of a central government, with the power to tax and to regulate commerce, was a virtual invitation to a new tyranny. Simply put, to men like Virginia's Richard Henry Lee and New York's Melancton Smith, the cure being offered was worse than the disease.

Each of these Antifederalist arguments gained some traction among the men attending the state ratifying conventions. But, as Madison and other Federalists had feared, it was concern over the lack of a bill of rights that quickly brought focus and cohesion to the Antifederalist campaign. The conviction that power could and would corrupt all men ran deep in the psyches both of men who favored and of men who opposed the Constitution. It had been a leitmotif of the Philadelphia convention, where delegates labored to grant powers to each branch of government but to hem in those powers through an elaborate system of checks and balances. Although supporters of the Constitution offered assurances in speeches and in the extended essays of *The Federalist Papers* that these restraints were enough to preserve the people's liberties, doubts had quickly mounted.

Had the men at the Philadelphia convention conspired to establish a tyranny—or had they simply lacked the will or wisdom to prevent a tyranny from emerging? Antifederalists could not decide. But the refusal to include an explicit declaration of protection for basic common law rights as well as critical natural and historically secured rights such as freedom of the press and liberty of conscience was a warning bell in the night that they would not ignore.

For hard-line Antifederalist leaders, this question was academic. Their goal went beyond the addition of a bill of rights; they sought the defeat of the Constitution itself. If they could not defeat the proposed new government, they were determined to propose alterations that would severely diminish its powers. The amendments they would propose at many of the ratifying conventions revealed their purpose: these were not simply amendments to secure the people's liberties; they were amendments to restore the supremacy of the states.

III

———

The Antifederalist leaders wasted no time sounding the alarm about the dangers to the people's rights posed by the proposed constitution. In October 1787, Virginians George Mason and Richard Henry Lee each published stinging critiques of the Constitution, turning the spotlight on this lack of a bill of rights. But Federalists responded quickly and forcefully to any suggestion that the Constitution would endanger Americans' rights. In a widely disseminated speech, Pennsylvania lawyer and jurist James Wilson reiterated the arguments made at the convention: first, the Constitution did not give the new government any power to interfere with personal liberties; second, to declare that specific liberties were protected was dangerous, for it suggested that the new government did have the power, after all, to decide which rights were guaranteed and which were not. In other words, a bill of rights would have the unintended result of enlarging rather than diminishing the powers of the national government. And, by taking the protection and restriction of rights and liberties away from the states, it would erode the very state sovereignty Antifederalists were so eager to protect.[1]

Alexander Hamilton picked up this same argument in the eighty-fourth of the essays written by him, Madison, and Jay, known collectively as The *Federalist Papers*. In this essay—written, as they all were, under the pseudonym "Publius"—Hamilton insisted that a bill of rights was redundant in a Lockean republic. Guarantees of rights, he declared, might be valuable as stipulations between kings and their subjects. But in a constitution "founded upon the power of the people, and executed by their immediate representatives and servants . . . the people surrender nothing, and as they retain everything they have no need of particular reservations." Indeed, Hamilton continued, the recognition of the people's rights was more emphatic in the Constitution's Preamble than in all the various state bills of rights. Echoing his fellow nationalist James Wilson, he argued that the inclusion of a federal bill of rights would be far more dangerous than its omission; it would "contain various exceptions to powers which are not granted; and . . . would afford a colorable pretext to claim more than were granted." Why, Publius asked, should we declare that things not be done when there is no power to do them?[2]

Wilson and Hamilton were attempting to make a public virtue out of the failure to include a bill of rights in the Constitution. Yet the Antifederalist leaders would continue to press the issue, for they knew that it tapped into widespread anxieties about the creation of what they called a *consolidated* government. Thus in the ratifying conventions, the lack of a bill of rights became the centerpiece of their attack. The genius of this strategy clearly lay in its ability to unify a disorganized opposition around a single, emotionally laden issue. In almost every ratifying convention, men proved ready to ask why there was no bill of rights—and to demand that one be included. Antifederalist leaders hoped this issue would derail ratification or, at the very least, open the door to proposals for other amendments designed to restore to the states the exclusive powers of taxation and regulation of trade.[3]

In the earliest conventions, however, the question of a bill of rights did not prove effective enough to defeat the Constitution. Federalists were heartened when, on December 7, 1787, Delaware became the first state to ratify it. Delaware's convention voted 30-0 in support of the new government, and the unanimity was easily explained: for this small, vulnerable state, a central government that regulated trade held out the promise of protection from exploitation by larger neighbors. Five days later, Pennsylvania ratified the Constitution, although the vote in this large, heterogeneous state was far from unanimous. When the Federalist majority refused to append the minority's dissent to the official report, the Antifederalists published it in the state's newspapers. On December 18, New Jersey, a victim of New York's greed, cast another unanimous vote for ratification. As 1788 began, Georgia and Connecticut joined the trend toward speedy and unanimous approval by the smaller states.

The compromise that gave each state an equal vote in the Senate had clearly quelled small states' fears. The only sour note came from Rhode Island, where a popular referendum rather than a convention defeated the Constitution. Although the leading Federalists were disappointed, few outside the state were surprised; "Rogue's Island," with its endless flood of paper money and its liberal voting requirements, was, for them, a perfect example of the perils of excessive democracy.

Two key states, Virginia and New York, posed the real challenge to ratification. Although Virginia issued its call for a ratifying convention on October 31, 1787, it was not until March 1788 that Virginians finally held elections for their convention. James Madison won a seat from his own Orange County, receiving 202 votes, more than twice the number of his two Antifederalist opponents combined. The choice of Madison was offset by the election of Antifederalist leader George Mason to a seat at the convention. In his campaign speech to the Fairfax County voters, Mason made his opposition to ratification abundantly clear. He also used the opportunity to provide a devastatingly unflattering portrait of his fellow delegates to the Philadelphia convention. "Fellow-Citizens," he said, "you have been often told of the wisdom and virtue of the federal convention, but I will now inform you of their true character—the deputies to that body from the states to the southward of us were *Coxcombs*; the deputies from Virginia you know pretty well; the majority of the deputies from the middle states were intriguing office-hunters; and those from the eastern states fools and knaves." Mason's blanket disparagement of the framers made one thing clear: the battle in the Virginia ratifying convention would not be a principled debate about political theory; it would be personal and potentially nasty.[4]

By the time the Virginia convention met, three more states had ratified the Constitution. But two of these Federalist victories came at a price. In Massachusetts, Federalists had been outnumbered and were forced to make a concession they had hoped to avoid. The sticking point here, as in Pennsylvania, was a demand for amendments to the Constitution. To avoid making ratification *conditional* on the inclusion of amendments, Federalists had to agree to support a long list of proposed changes to the new frame of government as soon as it was established. The Massachusetts compromise became a model for most of the remaining states: ratification would be accompanied by a list of proposed amendments to the Constitution. In South Carolina, for example, a proposal for nine amendments accompanied the convention's report of its ratification vote.

The Massachusetts model did not always appease conventions with strong Antifederalist contingents, however. In New Hampshire, where Antifederalists had a clear majority, the call for conditional ratification reemerged, threatening to produce a negative vote on the Constitution if amendments were not accepted before the government began to function. The only option for New Hampshire's Federalists was to push through a postponement of the vote. On February 24, their motion to adjourn until June squeaked by, 56 to 51. Only after news arrived that Massachusetts, South Carolina, and Maryland had ratified the Constitution were Federalists in New Hampshire willing to risk putting ratification to a vote. On

June 21, they won a narrow victory, 57–47. Here, too, Federalists had to agree to append a list of proposed amendments to the convention's report.

New Hampshire's vote made it the critical ninth state to ratify the constitution. This meant that the new frame of government had been officially adopted while the debate between Virginia's Federalists and Antifederalists continued to rage. It was not until June 25, 1788, that Virginia's Antifederalists bowed to the inevitable. After twenty-one days of intense debate, the leader of the Antifederal forces, Patrick Henry, conceded that his cause was lost. Shortly before the final vote was taken, Henry rose to address the convention. "If I shall be in the minority," he said, "I shall have those painful sensations which arise from a conviction of *being overpowered in a good cause.*" His good cause had lost, 89 to 79, but his side had wrung a concession from the victors that they would lay both a suggested bill of rights and twenty additional amendments before the First Federal Congress.[5]

New York proved even more difficult than Virginia for the Federalists. Opposition to the Constitution was so strong that New York did not elect delegates to its ratifying convention until April 1788. Here as in Virginia the struggle had been intense and the oratory incendiary. In a moving speech, Plattsburg lawyer Thomas Tredwell raised every Antifederalist fear and concern. "With this Constitution," he lamented, "we have departed widely from the principles and political faith of '76 when the spirit of liberty ran high, and danger put a curb on ambition." The proposed government, he added, offered no security for individual rights; equally disturbingly, it offered "no security for the existence of our state governments." After days of argument and debate, leading Antifederalist Melancton Smith proposed unconditional ratification—with one striking stipulation: his state could secede from the Union if its long list of desired amendments had not been acted on within six years. Alexander Hamilton, facing an Antifederalist majority in the New York convention, actually considered accepting Smith's proposition. He wrote to Madison for advice. The reply came quickly and decisively: no. "The Constitution," Madison declared, "requires an adoption *in toto* and forever." Hamilton thus held firm and on July 26, Federalists gained the narrowest of victories over their opponents. By a vote of 30 to 27, George Clinton's state had ratified the Constitution—but the Antis won the right to attach over thirty amendments to their declaration of support.[6]

The long list of amendments was humiliating enough for New York's Federalists. But it was the second concession wrung from them that sent waves of anxiety through Federalist ranks everywhere: the right to issue a circular letter to all the states, calling for their support in demanding a second constitutional convention.

The idea of a second convention was not new. It had been broached during the last days of the Philadelphia convention. In that instance, politics did indeed make strange bedfellows, for both nationalists and defenders of states' rights endorsed the idea. Defenders of states' rights like George Mason and Edmund Randolph hoped a second convention would result in serious alterations to the Constitution that limited the federal government's powers; but ardent nationalists like Gouverneur Morris hoped a second convention would be attended by men who were bolder than those gathered in Philadelphia and who would increase the scope and effectiveness of the government. The majority of the delegates, however, refused to even consider a second convention. Charles Pinckney of South Carolina saw nothing but "confusion and contrariety" springing from such a second gathering. If Philadelphia had proved anything, he said, it was the extraordinary difficulty of finding common ground among representatives of a dozen contentious, self-interested states. Should a second convention take place, it would be a scene of confusion and endless argument. The result, Pickney warned, was likely to be "decision by the Sword" rather than the pen.[7]

But if the proposal at the Philadelphia convention had died quickly, the idea survived. The New York circular letter had revived it. And in Virginia, Patrick Henry had snatched a small victory out of the jaws of defeat by persuading his state to demand that the first Congress call such a convention. Faced with such a prospect, a Federalist like James Madison was likely to consider amendments proposed and passed by the First Federal Congress the lesser of two evils.

By summer's end, 1788, only North Carolina and Rhode Island remained in limbo—neither foreign countries nor full members of the United States. On September 13, 1788, the Confederation Congress officially recognized the ratification of the new Constitution. Madison and the Federalists had won what seemed, on paper, to be a resounding victory. But a closer look suggested that a full celebration was not yet in order. Federalists still needed to win the loyalty of the farmers, merchants, and planters who viewed the Constitution as a mistake. They needed to fend off efforts in the First Congress to alter the Constitution and restrict its powers. And they needed to put to rest any notion of a second convention. To do these things, they must force the Antifederalists into full retreat.

IV

———

Instead of celebrating victory, James Madison anxiously awaited the opposition's next move. Like other worried Federalists, he was certain that the men fighting for Patrick Henry's "good cause" were not resigned to defeat. And he feared they had reason to be hopeful. Seven of the state ratifying conventions had explicitly called for amendments to the Constitution. Fortunately for the Federalists' cause, most had not made ratification conditional on the addition of amendments. North Carolina, however, had demurred. That state would not agree to join the new union until amendments were in place.

What troubled Madison most, however, was the revival of calls for a second constitutional convention. As early as November 2, 1788, he had laid out his fears of a second convention clearly and concisely in a letter to a fellow Virginia planter, George Lee Turberville. A second convention, he explained, would assume it had more latitude than Congress to amend the system. It would therefore "give greater agitation to the public mind." Madison was certain that—in contrast to the wise and responsible men who had gathered in Philadelphia for the first constitutional convention— the most violent partisans on both sides would seek election as delegates to the second one. As a result, the delegates would be, in Madison's judgment, "individuals of insidious views, who under the mask of seeking alterations popular in some parts but inadmissible in other parts of the Union might have a dangerous opportunity of sapping the very foundation of the fabric." As a veteran of the first convention, Madison assured Turberville that his fears were well founded. "Having witnessed the difficulties and dangers experienced by the first Convention . . . I should tremble for the result of a Second." [1]

Madison firmly believed, and conveyed to every sympathetic ear, that the "individuals of insidious views" were determined to use a second convention to "carry out their schemes." Those schemes, he told Edmund Randolph, went far beyond the campaign to add amendments protecting individual liberties and rights. The alterations desired by the Antis amounted to an evisceration of the national government's authority. Should the Antis succeed in their goal, Madison told Thomas Jefferson, they would "essentially mutilate the system, particularly in the article of taxation." The prospect of a second convention thus confirmed Madison's belief that Federalists had a better chance of controlling the content of amendments if they were proposed in the First Congress rather than outside it. [2]

George Washington shared Madison's concern that the Antifederalist threat was far from over. He, too, was convinced that a second convention would attempt to cripple the new government. It was clear, he told retired Maryland physician James McHenry on July 31, 1788, "That some of the leading characters among the Opponents [of] the proposed government have not laid aside their ideas of obtaining great and essential changes, through a constitutional opposition, [as they term it]." Washington's fears ran even deeper, for he did not rule out extralegal efforts to sabotage the new government. There was a danger, he warned McHenry, that "others will use more secret and, perhaps, insidious means to prevent its [the new government's] organization." That August he wrote to General Benjamin Lincoln, the man responsible for putting down Shays's Rebellion, that he feared a conspiracy was afoot. "I wish I may be mistaken in imagining, that there are persons, who, upon finding they could not carry their point by an open attack against the Constitution, have some sinister designs to be silently effected." To Washington, the situation was "a political shipwreck," and there seemed to be no star to guide the nation safely into port.[3]

To Federalists like Washington and Madison, the Antifederalists who clamored for a new convention were playing dangerously with the fate of the young, fragile republic. These men appeared blind to the fact that organizing and conducting such a convention would be fraught with questions and problems. How would delegates be selected? Would each state hold yet another convention to choose the delegates to this national convention? Would its agenda be confined to the amendments proposed by the ratifying conventions—or would new state conventions add new demands? A rough count put the number of amendments already proposed at over two hundred; even when repetitions were discounted, there were a hundred amendments on the table, most of them threatening to restrict the government's powers severely.

Federalists did not believe the nation could endure added months or years of uncertainty about the shape of the American government. Even the briefest delay in finalizing the government's role in regulating trade, raising revenues, and ensuring social stability would jeopardize America's ability to borrow much-needed funds from abroad. And if a second convention managed to strip that government of the powers the framers had given it, Federalists feared the nation would not survive.

Calmer heads than Washington's and Madison's might have realized that the Antis' schemes, especially the idea of calling a second convention, lacked sufficient popular or legislative support for success. Despite the strong Antifederalist presence in Pennsylvania, for example, that state refused to join in New York's demand for a second convention. Maryland and Delaware, both under tight Federalist control, also rejected the call. From New England, word came that New Hampshire and Massachusetts had both said no. With only three states willing to respond favorably to the New York circular letter, the convention proposal seemed to have died on the vine.[4]

Nevertheless, as long as the government's future was uncertain and its powers were untested, influential Federalists continued to worry. As appointments to the first Senate and elections to the first House got under way, the nightmare of a second convention gave way to the fear of an Antifederalist sweep of congressional seats. If the Antis won control of Congress, they could accomplish their goals without a convention. They could see to it that Congress would initiate the amendments and the alterations they desired. Antifederalists realized this as well. Thus, during the fall of 1788 and the winter of 1789, both sides geared up for battle. Madison summed up the danger dramatically for Washington and Hamilton. If the Antis failed in their plan to call a second convention, he wrote, they could accomplish their goals by getting "a Congress appointed in the first instance that will commit suicide on their own Authority."[5]

Virginia was once again a primary battleground and James Madison was in danger of being one of its significant casualties. His name had come up immediately as a potential Senate appointee. But little Jemmy proved a reluctant candidate at best. Practical concerns influenced his attitude, for he believed the Senate would be filled with men of wealth far in excess of his own. It would strain his budget to maintain the lifestyle expected of the upper chamber. More important, as a senator he would be answerable to and dependent on a Virginia legislature dominated by implacable foes of the Constitution. The issue proved academic when Richard Henry Lee and William Grayson, both stalwart Antis, were tapped to represent the state in the Senate.[6]

Madison's pride might have been ruffled by this rejection, but a seat in the upper chamber had never been his goal. He wanted to serve in the House of Representatives where revenue bills and other substantial legislation would originate. Patrick Henry, however, was eager to thwart Madison's ambition. Using his considerable influence over the Virginia government, Henry saw to it that the boundaries of the state congressional districts were drawn to Madison's distinct disadvantage. Madison's home county, Orange, was joined to several counties where Antifederalist sentiment prevailed. And, to make sure that Madison could not stand for election from a district more sympathetic to his views, the Virginia assembly—which was dominated by Henry—ruled that a candidate must reside in the district where he ran. Henry also arranged for Madison to be reappointed to the lame-duck session of the Confederation Congress. Madison thus felt it necessary to remain in New York City while his opponent, the young James Monroe, was free to campaign for the House seat. A war hero and a respected figure in Virginia, Monroe was an inspired choice by the opposition.

Henry's maneuvering lacked subtlety, and its purpose was clear to Madison's supporters. As Virginia lawyer Edward Carrington put it in a letter to his good friend Jemmy Madison, the "Anti's have leveled every effort at you." Henry's desire to see Madison defeated may have simply been revenge, for Madison had bested him in the ratifying convention. But Henry was an experienced politician and strategist. He realized that the Federalists' smartest move would be to take the offensive in the first Congress. They could steal the Antis' thunder by proposing the addition of a bill of rights to the Constitution. And, Madison was the likely man to shepherd the project through. Whatever personal satisfaction Henry might gain from seeing his foe defeated, his main objective was obvious: to prevent or delay the Federalists from neutralizing the Antis' most effective political weapon.[7]

The election for the House seat was set for February 2. Madison, who had little taste for campaigning, wrote to Edmund Randolph in late November 1788 that his friends were urging him to return to Virginia in order to counteract "the machinations against my election." Although he had, he told George Washington, "an extreme distaste to steps having an election-eering appearance," he knew he had to overcome his personal reluctance and take to the stump. His election was necessary to ensure that Virginia would not send to Congress another Virginian who supported those serious alterations to the Constitution that would limit the government's powers.[8]

There was no personal animosity between the two candidates, yet the stakes were high and their campaigns were hard-hitting. Monroe alleged that Madison had such an absolute devotion to the Constitution that "Not a letter of the Constitution cou'd be spared." This charge exposed the Federalists' dilemma: how could they defend the Constitution as it was written yet concede the need for some amendments? For Madison, the only solution was to publicly declare his support for rights amendments.[9]

In a letter to an influential Baptist minister, George Eve, Madison asserted that he had "never seen in the Constitution as it now stands those serious dangers which have alarmed many respectable Citizens." Because of this, he opposed any alterations as long as it remained unratified, especially those "calculated to throw the States into dangerous contentions, and to furnish the secret enemies of the Union with an opportunity of promoting its dissolution." Circumstances, however, had changed. With the Constitution now established, Madison saw no reason to oppose amendments that guaranteed the people's rights and liberties. What was more, he promised to champion these amendments "if [they were] pursued with a proper moderation and in a proper mode." The value of these amendments was clear to him; they would "serve the double purpose of satisfying the minds of well meaning opponents, and of providing additional guards in favour of liberty."[10]

Madison took every opportunity to publicly express his hope that the First Congress would propose these rights amendments. Yet privately, Madison voiced doubts that they would have much effect. He confided to Thomas Jefferson that he had little faith in such "parchment barriers" to the abuse of rights. Nevertheless, he stood ready to personally champion a bill of rights on the floor of the House if this would reassure "well meaning opponents" that the Constitution posed no threat to individual liberties. Madison's concern for well-meaning opponents exposed his political goal: he hoped to drive a wedge between these reasonable critics of the new government and those states' rights extremists who sought to rob the Constitution of essential powers. He had clearly decided that a bill of rights, carefully limited to individual liberties and with no alterations to the structure of government, was the way to crush the opposition.[11]

During his campaign, Madison stressed his support for "the rights of Conscience in the fullest latitude." This position had broad appeal among Virginia's minority religious groups, especially the Baptists. In his letter to George Eve, Madison gave assurances that the free exercise of religious preference would be a priority in his list of proposed amendments. His strategy proved effective. When the votes were counted, James Madison had won a seat in the First Congress, garnering 1,308 votes to Monroe's 972.[12]

Despite the intensity of the Monroe-Madison campaign, less than half of those eligible in the district had cast a vote. Clearly some Americans, weary of politics, were willing to give the new government a chance to prove itself, and eager to return to their more pressing personal concerns.[13]

In the aftermath of Madison's victory, there were men on both sides of the conflict who pondered his motives for declaring his support for amendments to the Constitution. Was this mere expediency, a promise made to secure his election and save his own political career? Was it vindictive, a determination no less intense than Patrick Henry's to win by crushing the opposition? Certainly Madison took his campaign promise seriously. Just as certainly, he, like his political enemy Patrick Henry, recognized that amendments proposed by a Federalist would be likely to steal the thunder of the Antis. And even more certainly, he understood that proposing these amendments himself gave him the best chance to confine them to matters of individual rights rather than structural changes.

Madison felt no shame in embracing the partisan politics that prompted this strategy. In *Federalist* 10, he had made clear his belief that factions, or differences of opinion and policy, were a fact of life. But he firmly believed that, for the republic to survive, these factions had to operate *within* the context of the established government. Men of all political persuasions had to be loyal to their country's Constitution. In the early months of 1789, Madison was not confident that the Antifederalists had this necessary loyalty, and thus he felt that they remained a threat to the republic.

Yet partisan political considerations, important though they may have been, cannot fully explain Madison's slow but steady shift toward support of amendments. James Madison was blessed with a complex intellect, capable of integrating a variety of motivations toward a desired end. Before he could act on his promise to propose amendments, he had to be convinced that they would, in some significant way, benefit the civic and moral development of his nation. As his thinking evolved, he discovered and articulated this benefit.

The question before him was this: what purpose would a bill of rights serve besides the disarming of the Antifederalist threat to the Constitution? Where, that is, did the true danger to liberty lie—and how could a bill of rights protect against it? In England, declarations of rights such as the Magna Carta had their origins in a desire for protection against arbitrary actions by the king. But America had no king; the president's powers were carefully stipulated and restricted; even if the procedure for his election was imperfect, the chief executive did not derive his power from birth or bloodline. There was no analogy between a monarchy and a republic whose government represented the will of the people.

This sovereignty of the people explained why many Federalists believed a bill of rights unnecessary. During the battles over ratification, Federalists had argued that the Constitution *was* the nation's bill of rights. As Thomas McKean of the Pennsylvania convention explained, "the whole plan of government is nothing more than . . . a declaration of the people in what manner they choose to be governed."[14]

Yet Madison was not convinced that the supremacy of the people would eliminate all dangers to individual liberties or would protect the rights of all citizens—especially the rights of minorities. In *Federalist* 10, Madison had assured his readers that the diversity of opinion and interests within a large nation was not a negative but a positive condition; this diversity, he declared, could be a safeguard against the rise of a tyrannical segment within society. Yet he could not really assure his readers—nor himself—that majorities would not arise, making possible a particular type of abuse. For when a majority's passions were inflamed or when its sense of responsibility was dulled, it could deny the rights of a minority.

In 1788, a Massachusetts Antifederalist had reached this same conclusion about the source of danger to citizens' rights. Writing as Agrippa, mathematician and librarian James Winthrop declared a bill of rights essential to "secure the minority against the usurpation and tyranny of the majority." Yet, unlike Agrippa, Madison doubted that a bill of rights had the power to dispel the threat of majoritarian tyranny. He feared that no "parchment barrier," no matter how exhaustive, no matter how explicit, could protect minority rights against a determined majority. As he explained to Thomas Jefferson: "Wherever the real power in a Government lies, there is the danger of oppression. In our Governments the real power lies in the majority of the Community, and the invasion of private rights is *chiefly* to be apprehended, not from acts of Government contrary to the sense of its constituents, but from acts in which the Government is the mere instrument of the major number of the constituents." Jefferson countered Madison's gloomy vision by suggesting that rights amendments might control the tyranny of the majority if it was expressed through the House of Representatives. But

Madison was, and remained, doubtful that Congress would be the major conduit for majoritarian abuses. Here lay one of the chief differences between James Madison and the Antifederalists: they envisioned oppression arising from one or all of the branches of federal government; he saw it arising from the social and cultural majorities within the general population.[15]

By the time Madison headed to the First Federal Congress, he had come to a profound, and much broader, understanding of the value of a bill of rights: it might be able to directly shape—and regulate—the behavior of the community itself. If its contents were presented as "fundamental maxims of free government" then, over time, "as they become incorporated with the national Sentiment" they might serve to "counteract the impulses of interest & passion." In other words, as these maxims became a vital part of the nation's political culture, as they came to define American ideals and to stand as an American credo, the conscience of the majority would curb its impulse to oppress others. Men, Madison was arguing, could be shamed into behaving like angels.[16]

V

February and March 1789 were cold and cloudy in New York City, but the raw weather could not dampen the excitement: the new United States government was coming to town. This was not the first time that New York would serve as the seat of national government, because the Confederation Congress had also met in this busy seaport city of some thirty thousand. Nevertheless, the city's desire to show its hospitality was obvious as it hurriedly paved its streets, spruced up its buildings, and set its artisans and laborers to work to finish construction of Congress's home, Federal Hall.

Despite all its efforts at beautification, New York did not appeal to some members of the new government. Virginia poet and Antifederalist John Page far preferred Philadelphia. "This town," he said, writing home, lacked the "Beauty & Elegance" of the City of Brotherly Love. "The Streets here are badly paved, very dirty & narrow as well as crooked & filled up with a Strange Variety of wooden Stone & brick Houses & full of Hogs & mud." [1]

Page's criticism was harsh, but understandable. Life in New York was a challenge. Even in bad weather, city streets were filled with the noise of vendors hawking their wares, the clattering of wagons, and the sounds of raucous laughter and heated argument coming from its many taverns. Especially in warmer weather, the air was filled with the scents of rotting garbage and horse manure. Pigs still ran through streets and alleyways, and dirt and grime seemed to settle over everything. The assault on the senses was likely to prove unnerving to those congressmen accustomed to fresh country air, the smell of new-mown hay, and little but the songs of birds and the calls of barnyard animals to disturb the day's peace.

Congressmen like John Page may have been less than enthusiastic about New York, but New Yorkers were eager to extend their warmest greetings to him and to his colleagues. On March 4, the day Congress was scheduled to begin its sessions, city residents offered a noisy welcome. The *New York Journal* exuberantly announced, "A general joy pervaded the whole city on this great, important and memorable event; every countenance testified a hope that under the auspices of the new government, commerce would again thrive—the farmer meet a ready market for his produce—manufactures flourish—and peace and prosperity adorn our land."[2]

Unfortunately, there were few congressmen to witness this celebration, which included the hoisting of the flag at Fort George, the display of the federal colors at the top of the new Federal Hall, and the firing of eleven cannons at the Battery, one for each of the states that had ratified the Constitution. Massachusetts representative Fisher Ames reported to his friend John Lowell: "This morning, the Birth day of the federal Govt. was announced by the firing of guns, & ringing of bells. At twelve, we repaired to the City Hall, but could not form an House or Senate. Thirty would have made a house. Thirteen only attended . . . and little hope is had of forming the two houses till Monday next."[3]

Monday next came and went, however—in fact, the entire month of March passed, wintry and gray—and still neither house of Congress had a quorum. To some extent, the absence of so many congressmen and senators could be blamed on bad weather and slow transportation. Even the most illustrious political leaders were helpless in the face of the elements; wind, rain, dangerous seas, and poor road conditions were great equalizers of travelers rich or poor. Even if the weather was favorable, the journey to New York would be taxing. Stages or carriages took four days to get there from Boston, with passengers seated on uncomfortable benches from 4 a.m. until 10 p.m. each day. Nights were spent in roadside taverns where the prudent man kept a wary eye on his possessions as long as he could remain awake. New Englanders who came by coastal packets had to be prepared for bouts of seasickness, delays, and the terrors of the whirlpool waters of Hell Gate, where Long Island Sound and the East River met. Travelers from south of New York were likely to combine land and water transport, usually culminating in a trip across the Hudson River. Those who dared an all-sea route risked life and limb in gales and storms. Representative Elbridge Gerry's wife Ann summed up late-eighteenth-century American travel when she wrote to a relative: "After six days being on the road tumbling from one rock to another riding over the Ice for miles down a river & push'd in a wherry a cross another & every night enjoying the delightful comfort of a down bed with covering so narrow that it wou'd scarcely suffice for one much less for three we arriv'd in New York."[4]

But the empty seats in Federal Hall were not entirely the result of travel delays. Illnesses—ranging from attacks of gout to toothaches—kept some men from leaving home and deaths in the family delayed others. Political maneuvering accounted for many other absences. New York and New Jersey, for example, had intentionally dragged their feet about electing or appointing their congressmen.[5]

Delays caused by weather, illness, and local politics were understandable if regrettable. But the fact that some congressmen gave greater priority to their personal business than to the business of the nation was cause for resentment and alarm. Such self-interest appalled observers like the French consul, the comte de Moustier, who condemned the "general indifference to public service" that it reflected. In a letter published in a Portland, Maine, newspaper, an anonymous writer harshly condemned the men who chose personal gain over public service. "A member who is at home from any other cause than sickness," he wrote, "must feel guilty of a crime that ages of repentance, and hecatombs of sacrifices cannot atone for." [6]

As the weeks went by, those who trudged daily to Federal Hall only to have to leave again because no quorum could be met grew both embarrassed and angry. Pennsylvania senator William Maclay vented his anger to Dr. Benjamin Rush: "I never felt greater Mortification in my life," he declared, adding that "to be so long here with the Eyes of all the World on Us & do nothing, is terrible." Maclay couldn't decide what he resented more: absent senators or remaining in New York. Fisher Ames was less concerned than Maclay about his own comfort. Instead, Ames fretted over the government's loss of revenue with every passing day and the impact the delays had on its reputation. "We lose credit, spirit, every thing," he lamented to Boston lawyer and historian George R. Minot: "The public will forget the government before it is born." [7]

The situation grew so embarrassing that congressmen who had arrived were urged to write to absent colleagues, prodding them to make their way to New York as soon as possible. It was obvious, as Richard Bassett put it to the still absent George Read, that the "Minds of the friends to the Genl. Government seem much Agitated & Distressed on Account of the Tardiness of the Members in Coming forward." Former Secretary of the Continental Congress Charles Thomson put it more bluntly to Read. "What must the world think of us?" he asked, before making an appeal to Read's patriotism: "[T]he eyes of the continent will be turned on you. . . . I must therefore as a friend entreat you to lay aside all lesser concerns & private business and come on immediately." And by March 29, Bassett was openly pleading with Read to "come forward" so that the government could at last be "put in Motion." [8]

The first order of business for every arriving congressman was to find lodging in the city. If some managed to stay with friends or relatives, most had to be satisfied with boardinghouses or cramped tavern rooms. Men from the same state tended to settle together. Thus, congressmen from Delaware and Maryland lodged at Mrs. Dobiney's house on Wall Street, while members from Pennsylvania and Virginia, including James Madison, chose to stay at Vandine Elsworth's on Maiden Lane. But whether they roomed on Broad Street, Maiden Lane, or Water Street, those who were veterans of Continental Congress or Confederation Congress sessions held in New York were probably already steeling themselves for the heat and humidity that would lie ahead when spring gave way to summer.[9]

The month of March drew to an end, cold and rainy, and still there were not enough congressmen to make a quorum in either house. This embarrassing situation did not prevent political leaders or their friends and families back home from engaging in lobbying, however. Letters seeking government appointments and letters recommending men for government posts circulated throughout the month. And an attempt was already afoot to move the nation's capital out of New York. Congressmen from Virginia and Pennsylvania were waging intense campaigns to relocate the government to their respective states. The Pennsylvanians insisted that the seat of government ought to be more centrally located—perhaps in York County, or even Philadelphia. William Maclay believed that New Yorkers' fear that the government would abandon the city accounted for their "rancor and malevolence" toward representatives from his state, Pennsylvania.[10]

On April 1, a wintry day of rain and snow, the House at last had enough members to begin its deliberations. Despite Federalists' fears, Antifederalists had utterly failed to make the legislative branch their stronghold. The party of the Constitution had won control of both the House and the Senate. As James Madison reported to Thomas Jefferson, "the disaffected party in the Senate amounts to two or three members only . . . [and] in the other House it does not exceed a very small minority, some of which will also be restrained by the federalism of the States from which they come." Madison was largely correct; nineteen Federalists would take their seats in the Senate chamber, with only four Antifederalist or antiadministration men—Virginia's Richard Henry Lee and William Grayson, Georgia's William Few, and Pennsylvania's William Maclay. Maclay had been selected as a Federalist but he almost immediately deserted the pro-administration side. In the House Antifederalists faced a clear Federalist majority. The Antis had, in fact, suffered several dramatic and embarrassing defeats at the polls: in Massachusetts, the aging revolutionary Samuel Adams had lost his bid for a seat in the House to a thirty-one-year-old lawyer, Fisher Ames. Federalists had also captured three of the six seats allotted to New York in the House.[11]

Surveying the new Congress, Fisher Ames pronounced himself unimpressed by the men who would serve beside him in this first session of the House. "There were only a few shining geniuses," he observed to George R. Minot. Ames did not indicate who the "shining geniuses" of the House might be, but there were a few that others might consider obvious candidates for this accolade.[12]

Connecticut had sent sixty-eight-year-old Roger Sherman to represent it. One of the few influential political leaders to come from humble origins, this artisan turned lawyer and successful businessman was widely respected by men as diverse as Alexander Hamilton and Thomas Jefferson. "Father Sherman," as some called him, was a large man, with large hands and a stern demeanor, who appealed to common sense more often than to philosophy. Unlike Patrick Henry, who prided himself on his oratory, or Fisher Ames, who delighted in his own wit, Sherman delivered his wisdom simply and directly. He had been a presence at every defining political moment in the young republic's history from the signing of the Declaration of Independence to the writing of the Articles of Confederation to the drafting of the Constitution.

In addition to Ames—who no doubt counted himself among the shining geniuses—Massachusetts was represented by the irascible but brilliant

Antifederalist Elbridge Gerry. Gerry's willingness to serve in the House reflected an issue faced by a patriotic Antifederalist. He had been one of the few delegates to the Philadelphia convention who refused to sign the Constitution, yet he sought election to its First Congress. He explained his position to his friend James Warren in a letter on March 22. Musing first on the many sacrifices of time and money he had made in service to his country, Gerry then declared that "a federalist I always was, but not in their sence of the word, for I abhor now as much as ever the corrupt parts of the constitution." Yet, he continued, he was "bound in honor to support a government ratified by the majority untill it can be amended, for to oppose it would be to sow the seeds of a civil War & to lay the foundation of a military tyranny." His mission, as he understood it, was to serve as a watchdog, protecting the people's liberties from Federalist encroachment, just has he had protected them from British oppression in the decade before the Revolution. In the coming months, Madison and other Federalists would have ample reason to wish Gerry were less vocal in his political views. He would prove the most articulate, persistent, and—many would say—disruptive of the antigovernment representatives. William Ellery, a Rhode Island merchant and lawyer, would describe Gerry as "a restless creature," and few who sat through his many speeches on the floor of the House would disagree.[13]

New Jersey had sent one of its own most respected leaders, forty-nine-year-old Elias Boudinot, grandson of a Huguenot refugee. He was tall and strikingly handsome in his youth, but his physical attractiveness paled beside that of his beautiful sister, the poet Annis Boudinot Stockton. Boudinot's religious devotion would lead him to publish *The Age of Revelation* in response to Tom Paine's *The Age of Reason*. A true social liberal, Boudinot argued for the rights of African Americans and American Indians and he sponsored the education of several Indian students. One of these young men showed his appreciation and admiration for his benefactor by adopting his name. This younger Elias Boudinot became the editor of the nation's first newspaper to be published in Cherokee and English.[14]

Madison, of course, was Virginia's contribution to the ranks of the "shining geniuses," although Ames did not consider him exceptional. The fact that Madison was "a man of sense, reading, address, and integrity" did not impress Ames. He found Madison too sympathetic to the French, and thus "Very much Frenchified in his politics." Madison's failings were obvious to Ames: "[He] speaks low, his person is little and ordinary. He speaks decently, as to manner, and no more. His language is very pure, perspicuous, and to the point." Worst of all, Madison was "a little too much of a book politician and too timid in his politics." Madison's ally in the Philadelphia convention, Alexander Hamilton, agreed with Ames. In conversation with George Beckwith, Great Britain's first minister to the United States, Hamilton described Madison as "a clever man," but "very little acquainted with the world."[15]

Ames dismissed the great majority of representatives as altogether ordinary. They were sober and solid, not likely to "embarrass business" or engage in intrigue, but their only distinctions were "virtues of the heart" and "the habits of business." Other men, less judgmental than Ames, would not have damned the representatives with such faint praise. Like the delegates to the Philadelphia convention, these congressmen were part of America's elite in wealth, education, and political experience. With few exceptions, they boasted college education from Harvard, Yale, the College of New Jersey, William and Mary, and what would soon be called the University of Pennsylvania. Several had attended school in England and continental Europe, and at least three had been students at the University of Edinburgh, a center of Enlightenment thought and scientific inquiry. Over a third were lawyers; twenty-four members of the House had passed the bar. A second group drew their wealth from plantations and slaves, mercantile enterprises, or a combination of these. Over twenty-five members of this first House had served as officers during the Revolutionary War, either in their state militias or in the Continental Army, and two of them had been prisoners of war. Twenty-two had served in the Continental Congress or Confederation Congress, and at least ten had been delegates to state ratifying conventions. Finally, seven of the men elected to this first session of the House had been delegates to the convention that drafted the Constitution.[16]

Despite the education and political experience of the members of this first House of Representatives, John Adams's son, John Quincy Adams, felt none seemed to exhibit true charisma. Adams, who would regularly sit in the gallery during the House debates, confessed in his diary, "I did not perceive any extraordinary powers of oratory displayd." Perhaps, like Ames, the young Adams set his standards too high, for he lamented to a friend that "you might search in vain throughout the house, for the flashes of Demosthenes, or for the splendid illumination of Cicero."[17]

No Cicero or Demosthenes was needed to deal with the mountain of mundane tasks that required little oratorical skill. Rules had to be established. A speaker had to be selected, and clerks and doorkeepers appointed. Positions in the new government had to be acquired for friends, relatives, and influential citizens from home. Only when most of these chores were completed could the more pressing business of the legislature at last be tackled.

To demonstrate the role of the House as the representative body of the people, its members decided to conduct their business in public. It was a striking innovation: the galleries were open to all. Soon a day spent in the gallery became a major tourist attraction for women as well as men. The House went further, allowing reporters from newspapers of every stripe to attend and then to print all they could record of the debates. Eager newspapermen would create their own shorthand in order to capture as much of the discussions as possible and, on occasion, members of the House obliged these reporters with copies of their speeches. Newspapers across the country reproduced the reports of those lucky enough to be present in the gallery or on the very floor of the chamber. Although congressmen frequently complained that a paper was biased or that they had been inaccurately quoted, most agreed that informing the public was a worthwhile enterprise. Despite the popularity of this decision, the Senate would not follow suit. Its proceedings would be conducted in the secrecy that was traditional in the American politics of the day.[18]

House members were in solid agreement about the first session's agenda. The most important tasks they faced were the creation of a federal court system and the establishment of a profitable revenue system. Setting tariffs, imposing possible excise taxes, and fleshing out the Constitution's vague outlines of a judiciary were expected to occupy the representatives through the spring and summer months. These issues, as well as salaries for congressmen and the proper mode of address for the president, would quickly stir controversy and reveal regional divisions as well as philosophical disagreement. The most controversial debates, however, focused on where to permanently locate the federal capital. As John Peter Gabriel Muhlenberg noted to fellow Pennsylvanian Dr. Benjamin Rush, "the Subject most canvassd, is The permanent Seat of Congress"; and, as one observer noted, that contest, especially between Pennsylvania and Virginia, was likely to occupy much time and produce much "party heat."[19]

And what of amendments? April passed without any mention of them in the House although many Antifederalists, both within the government and outside it, assumed that the promises made by candidates such as Madison would be quickly honored. But Madison, like his fellow congressmen, seemed largely preoccupied with the discussions of imposts and courts— and like them, he was caught up in the excitement of the arrival of the nation's first president, George Washington.

Washington had departed his beloved Mount Vernon on April 16. His journey would take seven days, for everywhere along the route to New

York—in Alexandria, Baltimore, Wilmington, Philadelphia, and Trenton—he was feted by officials and greeted by cheering crowds. Representatives from both houses of Congress hurried to Elizabethtown, New Jersey, to welcome him, and a ceremonial barge waited to take him across the Hudson River to Manhattan. As it made its way to the New York side of the river, ships and barges patriotically decorated formed a colorful escort. Elias Boudinot, who had been chosen to escort Washington to the city, described the scene to his wife, Hannah. "Boat after Boat & Sloop after Sloop added to our Train gayly dressed in all their naval Ornaments," he wrote. Boudinot estimated that the crowds waiting to catch a glimpse of the president were in the thousands. "The Streets," he said, "were lined with the Inhabitants as thick as the People could stand." Boudinot was particularly pleased to report to William Bradford Jr. that the ministers of France and Spain had waited on the American president. Theodorick Bland noted that great preparations had been made to receive Washington and his vice president, John Adams—including the sweeping of New York streets—and that there would be "something approaching *royal* Solemnity" in the addresses of congratulation. The excitement continued until, on April 30, Chancellor Robert R. Livingston administered the oath to Washington and the president's first term began in earnest.[20]

The month of May began with an address by the president to both houses of Congress. The influence of James Madison, acknowledged by many to be Washington's chief adviser, was evident in this address. Astute observers might have noted that Madison was laying the groundwork for amendments here, for, at his urging, the president included an endorsement of those changes to the Constitution desired by the people. Washington declined to make any specific suggestions; instead, with his usual political delicacy, he reminded the legislature that Article 5 of the Constitution placed the power—and the burden—of proposing amendments on their shoulders exclusively. It was up to them to determine the degree of public "inquietude" on which any amendment was based.[21]

Madison believed there was a considerable degree of popular inquietude, yet hard-line Antis seemed unwilling to press the issue. Veteran politicians like Patrick Henry understood that as long as "our highest toned Federalists say we must have amendments," the Antis should do nothing to assist them. He knew that a bill of rights sponsored by Federalists, and approved by a Federalist-dominated Congress, would go far toward isolating the Antifederalist leaders from their rank-and-file supporters. He also knew that any amendments proposed by Federalists would stop far short of imposing serious limitations on the federal government's powers. As Henry put it in a letter to William Grayson, "direct Taxation Treatys Trade &c &c" would not be addressed.[22]

Henry was wrong, however, in assuming there was a Federalist rush to propose amendments. In fact, many members of the pro-administration party believed their sweep in the first congressional election, coupled with the low voter turnout in many districts, meant that voters of all stripes had decided to give the new government a chance to prove itself. As far as they were concerned, the Antifederalist threat was over—and thus any discussion of a bill of rights would be a waste of time. In a letter to Thomas Jefferson, the wealthy planter Ralph Izard, a Federalist senator from South Carolina, impatiently dismissed any thought of amendments: "I hope we shall not be wasting time with Idle discussions about amendments of the Constitution; but that we shall go to work immediately about the Finances & endeavour to extricate ourselves from our present embarrassed, & disgraceful situation." Fisher Ames was equally adamant on the subject. "The revenue and judiciary cannot be postponed," he declared to Boston lawyer William Tudor, adding with his usual flourish, "they are the law and the prophets of our government, and perhaps every government."[23]

Federalist leaders outside Congress were also opposed to spending time and energy on amendments. Edmund Randolph, firmly in the Federalist camp once again, shared the general sanguine view that the constitutional crisis had passed. Even in Virginia, he assured Madison, "There is a great calm of politicks. The discontented themselves seem willing to wait with temper." Congregationalist minister Ezra Stiles expressed the widely held Federalist sentiment to Connecticut senator William Samuel Johnson that there should be "no Amendmts. made these 20 years; or not until by Experience & cool Judgt. we should be able to discern what Amendmts. are necessary. The Constitution is so good & excellent," he added, "that I do not wish to have it shaken by any speedy Alterations." Ezra Ripley, also a Congregationalist minister, waxed lyrical about popular sentiment in support of the Constitution in a letter to Representative George Thatcher. Referring to New England's 1786 farmers' revolt known as Shays's Rebellion, he observed with relief, "The horror excited in our minds by the late spirit of insurrection, flees away before the New Congress, like the darkness of the night before the rising Sun."[24]

James Madison disagreed with this sentiment. He remained as certain in 1789 as he had been in 1788 that, although the Antifederalists had been defeated at the polls, there were powerful men determined to weaken the federal government. He also remained certain that he knew how to stop them. All the Federalists had to do to put the last nail in the Antis' coffin was pass a bill of rights.

Madison spelled out the benefits of a Federalist-sponsored bill of rights to several correspondents. Writing to Samuel Johnston, he ticked off the gains to be enjoyed from this strategy: it will help bring the two remaining states into the union; it will fortify popular support for the success of the new government; and, hopefully, it will establish principles that might curb the majority's impulse to abuse the minority.[25]

Convinced he was correct in his assessment of the threat, and in the efficacy of his solution, Madison decided to act. On May 4, although the House was preoccupied with revenue estimates, he rose on the floor to announce his intentions: he would commence a discussion of amendments in three weeks' time, on May 25. The three-week delay would give him time to carefully prepare his presentation. This would, he hoped, ensure that he could orchestrate the discussion of amendments just as he had orchestrated the discussion of a new government at the constitutional convention.

Madison's preparation was characteristically thorough. He sorted and categorized all the amendments relating to liberties and rights that had been proposed by state ratifying conventions, and gave each a weight based on the number of times it had appeared. By this process, he distilled over a hundred into nine proposals, which together covered forty-two distinct rights. He added only two new restrictions on governmental power not mentioned by the states: the first would specifically prohibit the federal government from seizing private property for public use without fair compensation; the second, and far more controversial, would broadly prohibit the state governments from infringing on their citizens' freedom of conscience, or the press, or the right to trial by jury in criminal cases. With this second prohibition, Madison the nationalist was reaching down to restrict state authority.

Writing to his friend Edmund Pendleton in April, Madison had sounded a note of confidence. "There will be no great difficulty in obtaining reasonable [amendments]," he had declared, adding with some measure of pride that those he had drawn up were, to his mind, eminently reasonable. But this time, the usually politically acute Madison could not have been more wrong.[26]

VI

———

The representatives' response to his announcement took James Madison by surprise. He had been prepared to deal with the possibility of Antifederalist opposition, but not with the almost universal Federalist annoyance and indifference that greeted him. Still busy with arguments over the impost—was the tax on Caribbean molasses too high or too low? Could cotton be exempted from any duty at all?—the House majority saw Madison's proposals as an unwelcome interruption of serious business.

Madison may have misread the response of the Federalists in the House, but there was evidence that he had read the temper of the Antifederalists correctly: their leadership was not ready to give up the fight. On the day after Madison's announcement, Virginia representative Theodorick Bland, a trusted ally of Patrick Henry, presented to the House his state's petition for a new constitutional convention. Bland moved that the House, acting as a committee of the whole, take immediate action on Virginia's request. If the House acquiesced, a precedent would be set and the floodgates would open to similar petitions from other states. If two thirds of the states decided to join this renewed call for a second convention, the Constitution required Congress to comply.[1]

For a brief moment, Madison seemed in danger of losing control of the amendment process. But the House members showed even less interest in

Bland's motion than they had shown in Madison's call for a discussion of his amendments. To head off any further attempts to bring state amendment proposals to the floor, New Jersey Federalist Elias Boudinot proposed that all such petitions should be made available to members but no action should be taken until the requisite two thirds of the states had submitted requests for a convention. The Federalist-dominated House quickly agreed. Thus, on the following day, when Representative John Laurance of New York presented his state's proposal for a new convention, it met the same fate as the Virginia petition.[2]

Despite the lack of enthusiasm for a discussion of amendments or for a new convention, Madison remained convinced that his proposed changes to the Constitution were essential to crush Antifederalist opposition. He had told Jefferson in March, "I hope and expect that some conciliatory sacrifices will be made, in order to extinguish opposition to the system, or at least break the force of it, by detaching the deluded opponents from their designing leaders." The House's firm rejection of efforts by Bland and Laurance did nothing to change his opinion.[3]

But Madison's fellow Federalist legislators were in no mood to make "conciliatory sacrifices" while revenue and judicial issues remained unresolved. Thus, on May 25, the House moved quickly to postpone the consideration of any amendments. The *New York Daily Gazette* reported that even most Antifederalist members of the House opposed starting a discussion that would "produce too much delay in the bills already before Congress." The message was clear: the people's rights would have to wait; the people's revenues required their full attention.[4]

Two weeks passed without further mention of amendments. But Madison broke his silence on the subject on June 8. Once again, he moved for the full House to consider amendments, and once again he met with immediate opposition from both camps. The arguments against the motion were familiar and predictable. It would be inexpedient to consider amendments,

Federalist William Loughton Smith of South Carolina declared, as long as matters of far greater importance such as the "great business of the revenue" had not been resolved. The *Daily Advertiser* reported that Georgia representative James Jackson, a Federalist, and South Carolina's Aedanus Burke, an Antifederalist, also challenged the propriety of entering "on such a subject till the government was perfectly organized and in operation." Jackson then sounded the theme that had appeared, and would appear repeatedly, in editorials and private correspondence: amendments were improper "before the constitution had been tried and experience had ascertained its defects." As Jackson put it, to propose cures when no illness was diagnosed would be "merely speculative and theoretical," an approach to politics that went against the grain of the practical men of the House. Jackson then urged the House to postpone any consideration of amendments until March 1790.[5]

Madison responded in what was, according to the *Daily Advertiser,* "a long and able speech." His motives in proposing amendments, he declared, ought to be obvious to all. Yet he willingly shared them once again. First, despite the ratification victory in eleven states, many Americans remained dissatisfied with the Constitution. These critics could not be ignored, for they included men "respectable for their talents [and] their patriotism" whose concern, though misguided, arose from laudable motives. Second, many of the people who are dissatisfied would gladly support the "cause of federalism" if they were assured the Constitution did not threaten their rights and liberties. "We ought not to disregard their inclination," he declared, "but, on principles of amity and moderation, conform to their wishes and expressly declare the great rights of mankind secured under this constitution." An assurance that the Constitution would protect rather than erode the people's rights would also pave the way for the two holdout states—North Carolina and Rhode Island—to join the union.

Next, Madison tackled two of the familiar criticisms of amendments. Was a *federal* bill of rights necessary, since the states had already provided these protections? Yes, he insisted; although some state constitutions included a bill of rights, others did not. And many of the protections desired by the people were missing from those that existed. "Would the enumeration of particular rights serve to disparage rights not so named?" No, he assured the House, for he had built protection against this into his proposals.

Madison also took particular care to defend the inclusion of his resolution number five, which reached down to restrict certain actions by the states. It prohibited a state from such abuses as passing bills of attainder, imposing ex post facto laws, and violating the freedom of conscience, the freedom of the press, or the right to a trial by jury in criminal cases. In Madison's view, government at every level should be denied powers that endanger these rights. To offset this challenge to state sovereignty, Madison took care to add his support for an amendment stating that the powers not delegated to the federal government were reserved to the states.[6]

Madison then addressed the philosophical imperative he had first introduced in *Federalist* 10: the necessity of protecting minorities against oppression by the majority. "The prescriptions in favor of liberty," he said, "ought to be leveled against that quarter where the greatest danger lies, namely, that which possesses the highest perogative of power." This dangerous power lay, he explained, not in the executive or the legislative department of government, "but in the body of the people, operating by the majority against the minority." A bill of rights was only a paper barrier against that oppression, he conceded, yet it had value nonetheless. It could set a standard of behavior, and establish principles that could "controul the majority from those acts to which they might be otherwise inclined." It could also have a "salutary effect" on the decisions of the courts, which would come to see themselves as the guardians of these rights.[7]

For James Madison, a federal bill of rights was not simply a political expedient, a means of placating the opposition's followers or silencing its leaders. Nor was it just a means of preserving a balance of power among the branches of government. It was the best remedy for the potential excesses of the majority in a republic.

Madison urged the House not to postpone the discussion of amendments again. To do so for any length of time, he argued, would be to raise suspicions that the legislature opposed protecting the people's liberties. With that, he offered his list of amendments and renewed his request that the whole House constitute itself as a committee in order to deliberate his proposals.[8]

Madison had been thorough. He had been logical. And he had used all his powers of persuasion. But his Federalist colleagues were unmoved. The discussion he wanted would be protracted, they complained. It was too early to know what defects would emerge in the Constitution, they said. Taking up the question of amendments was as likely to raise as to quiet popular apprehensions, they added. Delaware Federalist John "Jack" Vining put the matter bluntly: we must keep to the business at hand, and that business is getting the government operational.

Madison realized he had lost the moment. When it was proposed that the issue of amendments be sent to a special, select committee, rather than be debated by the committee of the whole, he capitulated, reluctantly agreeing to this motion. He asked only that Congress devote a single day, immediately, to discussing amendments. This would convince the world that the friends of the Constitution were as firm friends to liberty as those who had opposed its adoption. Surely, he added by way of enticement, this would go far toward persuading North Carolina and Rhode Island to at last join the union.

Madison had made a major concession when he agreed to see his proposals shunted to a committee. But that concession did little to soften the resistance to any discussion of amendments. In a long harangue, James Jackson attacked Madison's every argument supporting the need for a bill of rights. Jackson considered the very notion of such amendments to be an insult to Congress. "Let me ask gentlemen," the *Congressional Register* recorded him as saying, "what reason there is for the suspicions which are to be removed by this measure? Who are congress that such apprehensions should be entertained of them? Do we not belong to the mass of the people? Is there a single right but, if infringed, will affect us and our connections as much as any other person? Do we not return at the expiration of two years into private life, and is not this a security against encroachment?"

Warming to his argument, Jackson pronounced a bill of rights pointless. New York did not have one, nor did New Jersey, Virginia, South Carolina, or Georgia—was the liberty of their citizens less safe for this? he asked. And what rights did Madison suppose were in danger? Was the liberty of the press challenged by Congress? Had the newspapers not recently attacked a member of the House with impunity?

Jackson ended with a warning: such amendments would prove an embarrassment to the government. How will we appear to the great powers of Europe, he asked, if we alter our Constitution before the imperfections of the government are truly known? "Our instability," he concluded dramatically, "will make us objects of scorn."[9]

The sly Elbridge Gerry decided to take advantage of the mood in the House. It was well known, he began, that he had once opposed ratification of the Constitution without amendments abridging its powers. But, he confessed with mock sincerity, he had come to recognize the importance of an energetic government. What troubled him now was the Federalists' hesitation to exercise the powers that government had given them. Could his colleagues be afraid to offend the voters? We must squarely face the question of amendments, he declared, and we must not be afraid to reject all or any of them if we think it is the wisest course. What did it matter if the people regretted "the disappointment of their fondest hopes for the security of the liberties of themselves and their posterity; they would bow to our wisdom."[10]

Gerry was, of course, being both disingenuous and sarcastic. It mattered deeply to him if the people's fondest hopes for the security of their liberties were dashed—and he had made it abundantly clear that he doubted the wisdom of the men in Congress. And it was certainly one of his fondest partisan hopes that the Federalists would give offense by ignoring the states' recommendations for amendments.

Perhaps some of his colleagues misunderstood Gerry's thinly disguised attack on them, but Madison realized he had been outmaneuvered. He had little choice but to withdraw his support for a special committee and, though he risked defeat, to move that his proposals—and his alone—be adopted by the House. The House was willing only to refer his motion to the committee on the state of the union. There the matter stood until July 21, when Madison would be expected to raise the issue once again.

VII

———

Soon after his abortive effort in the House, Madison's amendments appeared in the newspapers. Throughout the rest of June and much of July political leaders across the country chewed over his proposals. Had Madison been privy to their correspondence he would not have been cheered by the sentiments expressed.

Massachusetts Federalist Fisher Ames wrote to Springfield lawyer Thomas Dwight on June 11 that "Mr. Madison has introduced his long expected Amendments." Ames had little that was positive to say about Madison's efforts. He conceded that the proposals were "the fruit of much labour and research," but added, "there is too much of it" for his tastes. He was even less generous when he considered Madison's motives. They "may do good towards quieting men who attend to sounds only, and may get the mover some popularity—which he wishes." Ames appeared equally unimpressed in a letter to his good friend George Minot. If Madison's proposals were a "great dose for a medicine" they were a poor remedy for anything alleged to be ailing the country. "It will stimulate the stomach little as hasty-pudding. It is rather food than physic. An immense mass of sweet and other herbs and roots for a diet drink." Pennsylvania merchant George Clymer used a similar medicinal analogy in a letter to the prolific Federalist writer Tench Coxe: "Like a sensible physician he has given his malades imaginaires bread pills powder paste & neutral mixtures to keep them in play." In essence these Federalists not only resented the distraction of amendments but also found them too mild to merit discussion at all.[1]

Georgia representative Abraham Baldwin did not impugn Madison's motives as Fisher Ames had done, but he did voice the commonly held opinion that amendments were a waste of time. Writing to the poet Joel Barlow on June 14, Baldwin made no effort to hide his irritation: "We are too busy at present in cutting away at the whole cloth, to stop to do any body's patching." Baldwin believed there was no serious opposition left; Antifederalism, he maintained, had vanished without a trace. As for Rhode Island and North Carolina, their hesitation to join the union was prompted by purely local considerations, not by the lack of a bill of rights. He was confident that they would "come right before long" without any help from Madison. Baldwin's fellow representative Thomas Fitzsimons of Pennsylvania summed up the general negative attitude toward the proposals when he declared them "Nugatory and premature."[2]

The rejection of Madison's master plan by his own party delighted Antifederalists like William Grayson. He could not help gloating to Patrick Henry about this response. Madison, he reported, was so embarrassed by the response to his proposals that once or twice he was on the point of withdrawing his motion altogether.[3]

Even men who approved of the principles embodied in Madison's bill of rights seemed doubtful that the amendments would prove effective. George Lee Turberville, a Virginia Federalist, raised Madison's greatest fear: that no paper guarantee of rights could protect the country should the people themselves lapse into total depravity. In the face of the people's loss of morality and virtue, he declared to Madison, "The Constitution with all its amendments will be ineffectual to protect (us or) our posterity from the Evils which will inevitably await them."[4]

Madison did receive some encouraging words from friends. Edward

Stevens of Virginia assured Madison that the people he had talked to there were very satisfied with the amendments. And another fellow Virginian, Fredericksburg lawyer Joseph Jones, complimented Madison for putting forward proposals that "are of such a nature as to be generally accepted." But, like many of Madison's critics, Jones confessed he did not think "declarations on paper" were ever very effective.[5]

These tepid reassurances did not offset the harsh condemnations of Madison's proposals and of his motives. It appeared that Federalists and Antifederalists alike saw his push for a bill of rights as an obvious political maneuver. Madison had, of course, opened himself up to this criticism, for he had frequently admitted, even boasted, that his proposals would take the wind out of the Antifederalists' sails without doing structural harm to the Constitution. His critics on this score turned to their own nautical analogy, taken from English satirist Jonathan Swift. In *A Tale of a Tub*, Swift described how seamen would fling out an empty tub in order to divert a whale from "laying violent hands upon the ship." To these critics, Madison's amendments were a political tub, thrown to a political whale. Some Federalists found the strategy amusing, though a waste of time because the whale had already been rendered harmless. But Antifederalists such as George Mason understandably resented it.[6]

Perhaps the harshest judgment of James Madison came from John Fenno, the editor of the Federalist *Gazette of the United States*. "Mr. M[adison] is universally acknowledged a man of the first rate abilities" Fenno conceded, "but there appears to be a mixture of timidity in his disposition, which, as he is so influential a character, I some times fear will be productive of effects, not salutary to say the least." Madison's personal failings aside, Fenno believed the insistence on amendments had done great damage to the public confidence in the government. Even worse, Madison had given an opening to those more "artful, unprincipled, & disaffected" men, who waited "with burning impatience for an opportunity to embroil & embarrass public affairs." In other words, Madison had reopened a Pandora's box that the election of the First Congress had closed.[7]

Fenno was not alone in commenting on Madison's shy demeanor; Madison himself would be the first to admit he lacked charisma. But he had always compensated for this failing by his thorough preparation and his admirable intelligence—and, perhaps most significantly, by his alliance with men of forceful personality like Hamilton or natural charm and wit like Gouverneur Morris. Knowing that he did not cut an imposing figure or speak with a confident voice, he had asked the confident, likable Edmund Randolph to present his Virginia Plan at the start of the constitutional convention. Yet he had no ready and reliable allies in the campaign for amendments. His comrades in arms from the Philadelphia convention were scattered. Hamilton, anticipating an appointment to the Treasury department, was busy preparing his plans for the financial stability and economic trajectory of the country. Randolph was still in Virginia. The silver-tongued and wickedly witty Gouverneur Morris was in France. The much respected James Wilson would eventually become part of the federal government with an appointment as an associate justice of the Supreme Court, but for the moment he was a professor at the College of Philadelphia. Thus Madison stood starkly alone, facing down friends and enemies alike. Whether this was by choice, or from a failure to gauge the resistance he would face, or because no new allies were willing to present themselves is unclear. Whatever the cause, Madison was suffering the consequences.

Madison's suffering would grow more intense as the weeks dragged on. June 21 was technically the longest day of the year, but for James Madison, July 21 must have seemed to last far longer. On that hot summer day he rose to propose once again that the House resolve itself into a committee of the whole to consider the subject of amendments. This time, after enduring almost two months of direct and indirect criticism, Madison was more prepared for opposition than he had been in May.[8]

The response to his proposal was immediate—and again, it was discouraging. Fisher Ames, who was emerging as Madison's Federalist bête noire, countered with a motion of his own: let us turn the matter over to a special committee made up of one member from each state. Shunting Madison's proposals to a committee was bad enough; but Ames's motion went further. The committee should not be limited to consideration of Madison's proposals alone, Ames said. Instead it should consider all the amendments offered by the state ratifying conventions. This would mean that Madison's painstaking selection and editing of the many state proposals would be for naught. Far worse, from Madison's perspective, it would open the door to discussions of amendments designed to alter the structure and diminish the powers of the new government.

Ironically, the debate over whether, and how, to delay a long discussion of amendments occupied the entire day. This led Theodore Sedgwick to doubt that the creation of the committee would save the House any time. Any culling of the state proposals by the committee would be pointless, he observed, for each House member was certain to champion all the amendments that came from his own state anyway. Roger Sherman was more dismissive. He saw no reason for a committee and no need to discuss amendments at all. He repeated his now familiar argument that Article 5 of the Constitution was intended only to facilitate amendments that experience proved necessary. As yet, he reminded his colleagues, there was no experience to rely on. If the House proposed amendments based on "mere speculative points," he was confident the states would sensibly reject them.

When Elbridge Gerry rose to speak, it was clear that he had a very different agenda from these Federalists. He was eager to see the House consider the structural and substantive amendments proposed by the states, but he did not want their fate to rest with a committee appointed by the Federalist majority. To get around this roadblock, Gerry urged that any of the state proposals ignored by the committee should be brought forward to the full

House for consideration. "Any attempt to smother the business, or prevent a full investigation," he warned, "must be nugatory." To Fisher Ames, Gerry's purpose was transparent. In frustration, he protested that this would be no different from holding another constitutional convention![9]

Back and forth the debate went, some House members insisting that a special committee was essential, others arguing that a committee of the whole was called for, and some expressing a desire to postpone the entire matter so they could get on with the important revenue and judicial business on their agenda.

In the end, a tired and no doubt out-of-sorts legislature voted, 35–15, to create a select committee. The members appointed were Delaware's John Vining; Georgia's Abraham Baldwin; Connecticut's Roger Sherman; New Hampshire's Nicholas Gilman; Pennsylvania's George Clymer; New York's Egbert Benson; Massachusetts's Benjamin Goodhue; New Jersey's Elias Boudinot; Maryland's George Gale; South Carolina's Aedanus Burke; and finally Madison himself, representing his home state, Virginia. Just as Gerry expected, the committee composition reflected the dominance of Federalists in the House: only Aedanus Burke had cast his vote against ratification of the Constitution in his state's convention.[10]

It took this Committee of Eleven, as the select committee came to be called, only a week to deliberate and prepare its report. On July 28, as the heat of the summer deepened, Jack Vining presented the committee's work to the House. Overall Madison's original proposals, including his intention to insert the amendments into the body of the Constitution itself, had survived. The committee members had, however, seen fit to edit some of his prose and to rearrange the order of the amendments. And they had made a few substantive changes, including the addition of several guarantees to his nine umbrella proposals. These quibbles aside, Madison had every reason to be pleased. The general agreement between Madison's original proposals and the committee's report reflects both Madison's thoroughness and the dominance, on the Committee of Eleven, of Federalists who wished to avoid any substantive alterations to the Constitution.[11]

In his first proposal, Madison had intended to expand the Preamble to the Constitution by inserting the same principles, set down by John Locke, that Jefferson had relied on in his introduction to the Declaration of Independence. Madison's version was far less elegant, far more legalistic, and more long-winded than Jefferson's, however. It read:

> *That all power is originally vested in, and consequently derived from the people. That government is instituted, and ought to be exercised for the benefit of the people; which consists in the enjoyment of life and liberty, with the right of acquiring and using property, and generally of pursuing and obtaining happiness. That the people have an indubitable, unalienable, and indefeasible right to reform or change their government, whenever it be found adverse or inadequate to the purposes of its institution.*

In the Declaration Jefferson's stirring language justified a blood-and-guts revolution. Madison's blander prose presented an implicit justification of a purely political revolution that followed from the decision to replace the Articles of Confederation with a new government.[12]

The committee members, wisely, preferred a more succinct and far more limited addition to the preamble. Before the words "We the people," they proposed simply adding the most fundamental of Locke's precepts:

> *Government being intended for the benefit of the people, and the rightful establishment thereof being derived from their authority alone . . .*

But their omission of the statement on the right of the people to change their government was more than a stylistic decision. Like many Americans, these Federalists viewed with alarm the specter of repeated revolutions waged on the battlefield or at the ballot box under the Lockean banner.

Although Madison's intention was to preclude any amendment limiting the government's powers, he had been willing to alter the method by which the number of representatives in the House would be determined and regulated. His second proposal, which would have changed Article 1, Section 2, Clause 3, called for revising the rules by which the Congress could expand its membership. The Constitution provided that the ratio for representation was to be no more than one congressman for every thirty thousand people. It also stipulated, however, that every state would have at least one representative until an enumeration—a census—was carried out. If Madison's proposal passed, a maximum as well as a minimum representation would be established. Madison had left the key numbers blank, stating only that

> *there shall be one representative for every thirty thousand, until the number shall amount to___ after which the proportion shall be so regulated by Congress, that the number shall never be less than___ nor more than ___ but each state shall after the first enumeration, have at least two representatives; and prior thereto.*

The committee chose to fill in the blanks in Madison's proposal—setting the minimum of Congressmen at one hundred and the maximum at 175. But it rejected Madison's suggestion that each state be entitled to at least two representatives.

Madison's third proposal, to be inserted in Article 1, Section 6, Clause 1, was to add a restriction on the increase of House salaries:

> *But no law varying the compensation last ascertained shall operate before the next ensuing election of representatives.*

This proposal was tinged with the generally shared fear that those in office would succumb to the greed that was a fatal flaw of all men. The committee edited the language a bit but retained the principle that a sitting House could not vote itself a raise.

Madison's fourth proposal provided protection for the fundamental individual liberties and rights of citizens that most modern Americans as well as his contemporaries considered unalienable. The list was to be inserted into Article 1, Section 9, between Clauses 3 and 4:

The civil rights of none shall be abridged on account of religious belief or worship, nor shall any national religion be established, nor shall the full and equal rights of conscience be in any manner or on any pretext infringed.

The people shall not be deprived or abridged of their right to speak, to write, or to publish their sentiments; and the freedom of the press, as one of the great bulwarks of liberty, shall be inviolable.

The people shall not be restrained from peaceably assembling and consulting for their common good; nor from applying to the legislature by petitions, or remonstrances for redress of their grievances.

The right of the people to keep and bear arms shall not be infringed; a well armed, and well regulated militia being the best security of a free country: but no person religiously scrupulous of bearing arms, shall be compelled to render military service in person.

No soldier shall in time of peace be quartered in any house, without consent of the owner; nor at any time, but in a manner warranted by law.

No person shall be subject, except in cases of impeachment, to more than one punishment, or one trial for the same offence; nor shall be compelled to be a witness against himself: nor be deprived of life, liberty or property without due process of law; nor be obliged to relinquish his property, where it may be necessary for public use, without a just compensation.

Excessive bail shall not be required, nor excessive fines imposed, nor cruel and unusual punishments inflicted.

The rights of the people to be secured in their persons, their houses, their papers, and their other property from all unreasonable searches and seizures, shall not be violated by warrants issued without probable cause, supported by oath or affirmation, or not particularly describing the places to be searched, or the persons or things to be seized.

In all criminal prosecutions, the accused shall enjoy the right to a speedy and public trial, to be informed of the cause and nature of the accusation, to be confronted with his accusers, and the witnesses against him; to have a compulsory process for obtaining witnesses in his favor; and to have the assistance of counsel for his defence.

The exceptions here or elsewhere in the constitution, made in favor of particular rights, shall not be construed as to diminish the just importance of other rights retained by the people; or as to enlarge the powers delegated by the constitution; but either as actual limitations of such powers, or as inserted merely for greater caution.

Many of the guarantees Madison laid out conformed to traditions and expectations established by almost two hundred years of Anglo-American political culture. Some reflected an adaptation of the "rights of Englishmen" to the new experiment in republican government. But many of them also revealed the Revolutionary generation's persistent memory of the abuses arising from imperial policies in the 1760s and 1770s. Few Americans could forget that in 1760, James Otis Jr. of Massachusetts had lost a courtroom challenge to the British government's new Writs of Assistance, leaving the way open to arbitrary searches of cargo holds and warehouses and the seizure of goods. They would also have vividly recalled that in 1765,

Parliament had passed the first of two Quartering Acts, allowing the army to house its soldiers in American barracks and in public houses, and, if necessary, in inns, livery stables, alehouses, and the homes of merchants who sold liquors as well as in uninhabited houses, barns, and even outhouses. This act imposed two burdens on colonial communities: the disruption of daily life and the cost of housing and feeding the troops. Not surprisingly, there was resistance, especially when over 1,500 British troops arrived in New York City in 1766. In 1774, a revised Quartering Act became part of the collective punitive actions that colonists called the "Intolerable Acts." Together, these Intolerable Acts had carried the colonies to the brink of war. And every free American knew that the "shot heard round the world" was fired to protect the guns and ammunition the colony of Massachusetts had stored in Concord for the use of its militia. Thus, in stressing the protection of citizens against arbitrary search and seizure, in prohibiting the quartering of troops, and in securing the right of states to arm and sustain a militia, Madison had, in effect, written a condensed history of many of the central causes of the American rebellion.[13]

Several of the guarantees in this, Madison's fourth proposal, addressed the social and political realities of the new nation. Madison was aware that minority groups like the Baptists and the Moravians feared the impact of a nationally established church. At the same time, in states like Massachusetts and Connecticut where Congregationalism was established, the religious majority feared the loss of its privileged position to another denomination should a national church be created. Thus he stipulated that no religious denomination be established by the federal government. Similarly, Madison's decision to deny a protection against double jeopardy in cases of impeachment arose directly from the widespread concern that a president might abuse executive power just as a British king had done.[14]

Thus past and present, memory and immediate circumstances played their roles in Madison's selection of these guarantees. But the last paragraph in this fourth proposal served a special purpose: it was designed to put to rest any concern that an unalienable right not mentioned might be a right not enjoyed. Madison also hoped to make clear that the rights that were specifically mentioned were not chosen to stave off a looming threat of government abuse; they had simply been listed "for greater caution." Here Madison's didactic purpose surfaced: he wished to instill respect for individual rights in the minds and hearts not only of those who governed but of the majority they governed.

The committee retained the content of Madison's fourth proposal, though it edited the language to make the restrictions on the government more direct. It dealt a major blow to Madison, however, when it changed the last clause to read simply:

> *The enumeration in this Constitution of certain rights shall not be construed to deny or disparage others retained by the people.*

With the stroke of a pen, Madison's cautionary note had vanished.

Madison was probably more heavily invested in his fifth proposal than any other. It reflected his fear that, in the hands of the majority, state governments might run roughshod over the rights of minorities. Thus he proposed adding to Article I, Section 10, between Clauses 1 and 2, an explicit restriction on the states:

> *No state shall violate the equal rights of conscience, or the freedom of the press, or the trial by jury in criminal cases.*

If approved, not only would it go far toward protecting minorities; it would also be a blow to states' rights. To his relief, the committee approved this proposal just as he had written it.

Madison's sixth proposal, to be annexed to Article 3, Section 2, arose primarily from a desire to prevent burdening the courts with appeals of cases for small debts. It would set a minimum amount (which Madison left undetermined) as the threshold for an appeal. But it also sought to limit the reexamination of facts in cases in which a jury decision had been rendered. The committee accepted this proposal, filling in the blank left by Madison with the amount of $1,000.

Madison's seventh proposal, to be inserted in Article 3, Section 2, in place of the third clause in the original Constitution, dealt with the procedures for punishment of crimes and the maintenance of law and order. It guaranteed trial by an impartial jury for all crimes except impeachment, or those arising in land or naval forces or the militia when it was serving in wartime or in a time of public danger. The juries were to be composed of freeholders "of the vicinage," or community, in which the alleged crime took place. Conviction would require a unanimous verdict, and those convicted had the right to appeal along with "other accustomed requisites," that is, common law customs. In crimes punishable by loss of life or member, a grand jury indictment was necessary. In extreme circumstances—if the county was occupied by an enemy or caught up in an insurrection—the trial could be moved to a nearby venue. Crimes committed outside any county boundary were to be tried in a designated county.

Madison followed these procedural rules with a ringing declaration of the value of jury trials:

> *In suits at common law between man and man, the trial by jury as one of the best securities to the rights of the people, ought to remain inviolate.*

Madison's careful enumeration of the protections guaranteed to the accused and his emphasis on the virtues of trial by jury reflected a societal faith in, and commitment to, legal justice. But behind this proposed amendment also lay a long history of frontier insurrections and slave up-risings—those "public dangers" that disturbed men of property and men whose property included human beings. These revolts had revealed the sharp cleavages within American society between rich and poor, coastal residents and backcountry farmers, men with power and men whom slavery made powerless.

In the 1670s, a charismatic settler named Nathanael Bacon had led backcountry settlers, angered by the Tidewater planters' refusal to protect them from Indian attack, in a rebellion that shook the colony of Virginia. The rebels had managed to momentarily seize control of the colonial capital and only the sudden death of their leader had sealed the rebellion's fate.[15]

In 1764, Pennsylvania's frontier rebels, the Paxton Boys, frightened its genteel classes by marching on Philadelphia. Like the westerners of Bacon's rebellion, these backcountry farmers had been frustrated by the refusal of their colonial government to subdue the local Indians. When the Quaker-dominated government did not act, almost sixty "Boys" took vigilante action in the winter of 1763. In their rage, they chose to massacre a peaceful Conestoga Indian settlement that posed no threat to them at all. Then, six hundred frontiersmen armed themselves and headed to the colonial capital. Only the intercession of Benjamin Franklin and a promise of concessions to their demands persuaded the Paxton rebels to return home. In the end, the government did little to redress the backcountry settlers' grievances. But the events did end the long dominance of pacifist Quakers in the colonial legislature.[16]

In 1771, backcountry frustration with a coastal elite led to an uprising in North Carolina known as the Regulator movement. In both North and South Carolina, pleas by western settlers for government services and for representation in the colonial legislature had been ignored. On the eve of an American Revolution whose motto was "no taxation without representation," North Carolinians took up arms against the elite legislators who taxed them without allowing them a voice in government. The crushing defeat of the Regulators left a legacy of bitterness. Many of these poor farmers would fight on the British side in the American Revolution.[17]

But it was Shays's Rebellion of 1786 in Masachussetts that produced national political consequences. As the new nation struggled with postwar economic depression, Massachusetts farmers rose up against their state government. Angered by mortgage foreclosures and tax increases, these rebels mounted an attack on the state courts that issued the foreclosures. The protest spread, threatening to engulf all of New England. The rebels were routed by Massachusetts militias, but fear of similar uprisings by farmers or slaves tipped the balance in favor of calling a constitutional convention.[18]

These east-west conflicts revealed the class tensions that always seemed to bubble beneath the surface in American society. But antagonism was also a constant reality in a society that made race a basis for discrimination and slavery. Despite the ultimate failure of African American revolts on Long Island, New York, in 1708, in South Carolina in 1739, and in New York City in 1712 and 1741, every incident reminded slave owners that violent resistance was always possible.[19]

It was against this backdrop that the House committee endorsed Madison's seventh proposal. Once again, however, the committee members preferred direct language to Madison's somewhat convoluted phrasing. Their editing assured the accused of a speedy and public trial, of a clear understanding of the accusation brought against him, and of his right to be confronted with witnesses against him and obtain witnesses on his behalf. They also added an explicit right to "the assistance of counsel for his defence." The paragraph covering the venue for trials remained as Madison had written it.

With his eighth proposal, which would create a new Article 7 in the Constitution, Madison hoped to silence, or at least muffle, the criticism that the power given to the president was a prescription for tyranny by reasserting the separation of powers among the branches of government. Here, too, the committee made small revisions of language but not of intent.

Madison's final proposal, to which the committee agreed, stated simply that the existing Article 7 be numbered as Article 8.

It was this report by the select committee that the House, sitting as a committee of the whole, would ultimately debate.

VIII

———

On a rainy August 3, the House began its session with a message delivered by the secretary of the Senate. The Senate, he reported, had passed a bill providing for the establishment and support of lighthouses, beacons, and buoys. The concurrence of the House was requested. Next a bill for registering and clearing vessels and regulating the coastal trade was given its third reading and recommitted to the committee of the whole on the following day. Two additional bills received their second reading: one for establishing a land office in the western territory; the other to provide for the safekeeping of the acts, records, and seal of the United States. After these items had cleared the agenda, Madison moved that the report of the Committee of Eleven be debated by a committee of the whole on August 12. Without discussion of Madison's motion, the House moved on to its remaining business.[1]

Madison's success in getting the Committee of Eleven's report onto the agenda for August 12 merited little attention in letters that week. From Virginia, the Reverend John Brown wrote to Judge Harry Innes that he expected the House would agree to the report without any great alteration. And Roger Sherman told Salem Merchant Henry Gibbs that he thought the amendments would "probably be harmless & satisfactory to those who are fond of Bills of rights," but he still preferred that they be added as a supplement. With few exceptions, the correspondence to and from congressmen revolved around appeals for government positions, the appropriate salaries of representatives and senators, and the still unsettled judicial and revenue systems. The most controversial issue that week continued to be whether the president ought to have the power to remove appointees from office. The least controversial issue was the wish that Congress adjourn before the August heat became intolerable.[2]

August 12 came, as hot and uncomfortable as the days preceding it, yet there was no mention of the select committee's report. At last, the following day, after a vote on a bill relating to Indian affairs, Richard Bland Lee moved that the House form itself into a committee of the whole to consider the report on amendments. The days of debate that followed revealed how vivid the recent past remained for these veterans of political protest and of revolution. They laid bare the Federalists' anxiety to maintain the image of the Constitution as a carefully and deliberately considered document. They reprised the disagreement that lay at the heart of the Federalist and Antifederalist battles: who should speak for "the people," the state or the federal government? In these often disjointed discussions, long-standing quarrels and longer-standing resentments flared and the esteem, high or low, in which men held one another was exposed by the tone of many exchanges. As the days wore on and tempers wore thin, cracks would appear in the civility these men struggled to maintain.[3]

Predictably, challenges and complaints arose as soon as the discussion of amendments began. Both Theodore Sedgwick and South Carolina's William Smith sounded the now familiar reminder that the House had more pressing priorities. The representatives were, after all, still in the midst of discussions on congressional salaries and an act to finance negotiations and treaties with Indian tribes. While others cited legislative priorities, Pennsylvania Federalist Thomas Hartley introduced a refreshing, if spiteful, basis for opposition to a discussion of the committee's report. Although other

Federalists had come around to support a bill of rights, Hartley remained unshakably opposed. His reason was simply that he did not want to satisfy "the artful and designing" opponents of the Constitution by approving any amendments at all.[4]

Much of the resistance to taking up the amendments arose from the same source as at the Philadelphia convention: a collective yearning to go home. Representatives longed to leave New York City and the Spartan accommodations of local boardinghouses. With, as they hoped, an end to the session approaching, these men wanted to complete their work on revenue bills and the organization of the judiciary—and then adjourn.

Madison, who had endured crowded quarters, oppressive heat, and the presence of large, annoying flies at the Philadelphia convention, had little sympathy for his colleagues' desire to sleep once again in their own beds. He protested against any further delay, declaring that the subject of amendments had been postponed too long. He reminded the House that many voters fully expected Congress to produce a bill of rights. To adjourn without producing one would alarm the public. A chastened House reluctantly agreed.

Almost immediately, an old controversy returned: where should the amendments be placed? The select committee, like Madison, embedded them in the body of the original document. But many members of the House now sided with Roger Sherman, who had, from the beginning, insisted they be placed as a supplement to the Constitution. The usually plainspoken Sherman now argued with uncharacteristic eloquence for adding the amendments as a supplement. He urged the House not to alter by authority of Congress or the state governments what had been created by authority of the people themselves. Madison disliked the idea of a supplement, but he was willing to concede the point in order to bring this discussion to an end. He signaled his agreement to Sherman's position.

Still, the debate over how and where to place the amendments had not run its course. Several Federalists balked at anything that would tarnish the image of the Constitution as the achievement of men of unimpeachable patriotism and exceptional wisdom. Delaware's Jack Vining, for example, feared that placing amendments in a supplement would make the Constitution look like a letter written in haste, to which a postscript longer than the letter itself had to be added. Even more extreme outpourings of reverence and protection for the Constitution followed. Pennsylvania's George Clymer called the document "a monument of the wisdom and patriotism of those who framed it." Maryland lawyer Michael Jenifer Stone agreed that adding a postscript would imply that the framers' judgment had been defective.[5]

Stone's protectiveness brought Elbridge Gerry to his feet. Gerry, who had attended the Philadelphia convention, rejected Stone's concern for the "worthy" gentlemen who wrote the Constitution. Such admiration, he declared, was misdirected; praise properly belonged to the men of the state ratifying conventions.

As the debate threatened to drag on, Egbert Benson, a member of the select committee, attempted to intervene. The committee, he said, had considered this question of where to place the amendments and had decided against a supplement. Since the article providing for an amendment process appeared in the original text, the committee agreed with Madison that the amendments ought to be placed there as well.

Benson's attempt to close off the discussion failed. House members simply ignored his comments, and thus, by implication, signaled a willingness to ignore other decisions of the committee as well. The debate continued. Should the original document remain "inviolate," and not, as the *Gazette* recorded the always pugnacious James Jackson as saying, "patched up from time to time, with various stuffs resembling Joseph's coat of many colors?"[6]

Madison again took the floor, this time reversing himself and throwing his support once more to the incorporation of the amendments. But Roger

Sherman refused to abandon his argument that the will of the people, as expressed in the Constitution, could not be altered by Congress or by the state legislatures. The argument was faulty, and Elbridge Gerry knew it. Taking the floor, he pointedly reminded Sherman that the delegates to the Philadelphia convention had not been directly elected by the people—but the members of the House *had* been. Thus the House represented the will of the people more directly than the convention had, and amendments passed by the Congress and submitted to the state legislatures would originate from a higher authority than the Constitution itself. It was a brilliant argument—and difficult to challenge.

The power of Gerry's argument coupled with sheer exhaustion on the subject led the committee of the whole to defeat Sherman's motion. With that, the members returned with relief to their discussions of an act to establish the judicial courts of the United States and a bill to provide for the safekeeping of the acts, records, and seal of the United States.

The next day, August 14, the House went into committee once again to discuss the amendments. This time, the members addressed the content of the select committee's report rather than the placement of the amendments. The first proposal was the addition of a paragraph to the Constitution's Preamble asserting that the government rested on the authority of the people. No one, Federalist or Antifederalist, disagreed with Locke's theory of the social contract that made the people, rather than their government, the sovereign. Thus, despite some evidence of a lingering reluctance to tamper with the original text, the amendment passed.

The debate on the next proposal—which set a limit on the size of the House but assured each state of at least one representative regardless of population—moved reasonably quickly. After several changes were suggested, and voted down, this proposal also passed. The representatives, eager to avoid appearing greedy, then swiftly approved a third proposal that forbade a sitting House to alter its own compensation. With this small but encouraging start, the House ended its discussion of the amendments and turned its attention once again to the establishment of the federal court system.

Any satisfaction Madison felt that the debate was finally under way was soured by a scathing newspaper attack on his motives that appeared the same day. The author, Connecticut-born Noah Webster, had been a friend to Madison in the past, but now, writing as "Pacificus," Webster excoriated him for proposing amendments. First, he accused Madison of intellectual, and political, inconsistency: in an earlier House debate over the impost bill, he wrote, "you declared yourself an enemy to local attachments, and said you considered yourself not merely the representative of *Virginia*, but of the *United States*." Now, Webster declared, you justify your part in pushing amendments because you pledged to your Virginia constituents that you would do so. The accusation that Madison's nationalism could be readily sacrificed when it threatened his own political career surely stung. But this was not the only criticism Webster leveled at his friend. He also accused Madison of a sectional bias in claiming that the people clamored for a bill of rights. In his own travels across the country, Webster wrote, he found just the opposite to be true. The citizens of the northern and middle states did not want amendments, nor did they believe amendments would satisfy the opposition or bring stability to the government.

After impugning Madison's motives, chiding him for ideological in-consistencies, and accusing him of sectional bias, Webster closed Pacificus's essay with assurances that he meant no disrespect. He had always esteemed Madison's virtues and abilities, he told his readers, yet he felt compelled to condemn the waste of time that resulted from Madison's actions. A far better course, Pacificus declared, would be to win over the Constitution's critics and the uninformed with "reason and equitable laws" rather than by throwing them "an empty tub." Small wonder that Madison would soon describe the amendment issue as "difficult and fatiguing" and "exceedingly wearisome."[7]

On Saturday, August 15, the House moved quickly to a discussion of the Committee of Eleven's report. Elias Boudinot took the chair and the committee of the whole began its debate on the fourth proposal, which guaranteed that "no religion shall be established by law, nor shall the equal rights of conscience be infringed." Roger Sherman, who continued to see no reason to deny the government a power it had not been given in the first place, insisted that this article served no purpose at all. Sherman's logic may have been unimpeachable, but his political judgment was decidedly poor.

Freedom of conscience mattered to Americans. For members of religious minorities like Representative Daniel Carroll, scion of one of Maryland's most distinguished Catholic families, this guarantee was the most important the House would discuss. But members of denominations that did enjoy support in several states as established churches were just as invested in this guarantee. The establishment of a national church would deprive them of the support they received through local taxation.

Hoping to satisfy House members from states with established churches, Madison recommended that the word "national" be inserted before "religion." This would leave states like Massachusetts free to continue their support for designated churches. But the very use of the word "national" to describe the government created by the Constitution triggered an outburst by Elbridge Gerry.

It was not the larger issue of religious establishment that sparked Gerry's outburst; it was his lingering resentment over the damaging labels that had been used in the ratification debates. In 1787, Gerry declared, there had been men who actually wanted a *federal government*, yet they had been tarred with the label *Antifederalists*. The term *Federalist* had then been hijacked by men who wanted a *national* government. The proper way to distinguish the two groups, Gerry insisted, was by labeling them "rats and antirats." Perhaps Gerry did not mean rodents; perhaps the terms were only abbreviated versions of "ratifiers" and "antiratifiers." But Gerry's obvious resentment and anger revealed what Madison feared: for men like Gerry, Antifederalism was not dead; it had simply metamorphosed. The battle over the creation of a new government had been lost, but the struggle to define and confine its powers continued. The question was: were Madison's amendments a concession to this continuing strength of the Antifederalists or were they a clever means of crushing it? The answer was, and had always been, both; the amendments reflected that combination of "effort and sacrifice" Madison believed necessary to extinguish opposition to the new government.[8]

Madison did not want to cross swords with Gerry again. To avoid this, he withdrew his motion. In its place, the committee of the whole approved the more direct rephrasing suggested by New Hampshire's Samuel Livermore: "Congress shall make no laws touching on religion or the rights of conscience."

As the legislators moved through the proposals, Madison began to see a shift in the attitude of the Federalist majority. His persistence had ensured that amendments would be debated. And the resulting debates were moving Federalists to recognize the role a firm promise that certain liberties were inviolate could play in finally defeating opposition to the new government. This did not mean that harmony reigned, but it did suggest that Madison's perseverance was paying off.

As if to demonstrate that harmony would not reign under any circumstances, the next proposition prompted protracted and intense debate. This amendment pulled together several rights that Madison and most state ratifying conventions agreed merited protection: freedom of speech, freedom of the press, the right of the people to assemble, and the right to petition the government for redress of grievances. Few representatives, if any, would object to these rights. But a heated argument began when the Antifederalist Thomas Tudor Tucker moved to add that people had a right "to instruct their representatives."

With Tucker's motion, two very different notions of representation in a republic were pitted against each other. Many eighteenth-century political leaders, especially within the Federalist camp, believed that the hallmark of a legislator or executive was his right to exercise independent decision making. His election indicated the trust the community placed in his superior wisdom and knowledge as he decided what best served its interests. In 1789, Madison as well as Washington embraced this view. Both men looked with alarm at the growing tendency within their home state, Virginia, for legislators to pander to popular whim and to pass laws solely to ensure the support of voters. The result, Madison declared, was a stream of abuses "so frequent and so flagrant as to alarm the most steadfast friends of Republicanism."[9]

But for others, including many who would become supporters of Thomas Jefferson's Republican Party, the men chosen to represent the community were obliged to serve as conduits of that community's express desires and demands. It was not their individual judgment but their reliance on advice and instruction from the voters that defined the legislators' role. Both understandings of representation operated in America's governments; the question was which one the Constitution should endorse.

Thomas Hartley was the first to oppose Tucker's motion. "Representatives," the *Gazette* reported him as saying, "ought to possess the confidence of their constituents; they ought to rely on their honour and integrity." The practice of instructing representatives, he declared, was too often exercised in times of "popular commotion," when citizens resorted to the "prejudices of party," rather than heeding "the dictates of reason and policy." The *Congressional Register* recorded Hartley's conviction that the best government was "composed of men of firmness and wisdom to discover and resist the popular error."[10]

Virginia's John Page countered with an argument that proved to be nothing less than a redefinition of the entire purpose of the federal government. "In a government instituted for the sole purpose of guarding the rights of the people," he said, the right to instruct representatives was entirely proper. Indeed, the *Congressional Register* reported Page as saying, "Instruction and representation in a republic, appear to me to be inseparably connected." Both George Clymer and Roger Sherman disagreed. They reasserted Hartley's position that a legislature must be an independent and deliberative body—and they went further. The people, they declared, must not be led to believe they can control the debates within that body.[11]

Elbridge Gerry entered the debate with his characteristic sarcasm. To suppose we cannot be instructed, he said, is to suppose that we are perfect. As he saw it, giving the people the right to instruct their representatives would benefit rather than hamstring the legislators by providing "a fund of useful information for the legislature." "I hope," he concluded, "we shall never presume to think that all the wisdom of this country is concentrated within the walls of this house." Not only did Gerry support the right of the people to instruct their delegates; he supported making instructions binding on all representatives.[12]

Madison hoped to sidestep the issue of instruction entirely. He urged the House to confine itself to approving "an enumeration of simple acknowledged principles" and avoiding controversial and disputed ones. Smith of South Carolina and Stone of Maryland agreed. But Gerry refused to yield. He rose again, only to take his argument in a new direction. He began with a comment on human vanity, pointedly directed at the author of the amendments. He understood, he said, the reluctance of Mr. Madison to support additions to the proposals he and the committee had laid before the House. "It is natural, sir, for us to be fond of our own work, we do not like to see it disfigured by other hands." He, on the other hand, remained open to further deliberation and discussion on the subject; raising the stakes considerably, he reiterated his desire to see "all the amendments proposed by the respective states . . . considered."[13]

Gerry's attack on Madison had exhausted Jack Vining's patience. In an undisguised jab at Gerry, Vining observed, "If . . . there appears on one side too great an urgency to dispatch this business, there appears on the other an unnecessary delay and procrastination equally improper and unpardonable." As a member of the Committee of Eleven, Jack Vining could assure his colleagues that the issue of binding resolutions had been thoroughly discussed and rejected. As to Gerry's suggestion about considering all the state amendments, that issue was dead: the House had already accepted the committee's decision against reporting these state recommendations.[14]

Vining was clearly tired of Gerry's demanding attention by rising six or seven times to speak on any question. But Gerry just as clearly did not care. He soon rose again, this time to declare that he wanted no hand in amending the Constitution, but "if he must interfere he would," as he put it, "do his duty."[15]

And so the debate continued, until at last several members attempted to call the question. Even this did not bring the desired closure. A weary Virginian, John Page, sounded a note of frustration tinged with dark humor. He was sorry, he declared, to see gentlemen so impatient to end the discussion, especially as "very little attention [had been] paid to any thing that was said." Perhaps he was correct, for after several more extended speeches, New Jersey representative Thomas Sinnickson asked the chairman to remind him what question was under debate. The discussion had become so desultory, he declared, that he feared the topic had been lost sight of altogether.[16]

And still the debate dragged on, and again several members called the question. When the vote was at last taken, the motion to include binding instructions went down to defeat, 10 in favor and 41 opposed.

Fisher Ames now attempted to speed the process along by submitting all the proposed amendments to a formal vote of the House. To no one's surprise, Elbridge Gerry protested. He accused Ames of consistently trying to stifle debate and discussion, first by urging that the select committee be created and now by proposing an end to this more informal and open forum for debate. If his colleagues were tired of the discussion, Gerry said, they should postpone it until it can be taken up again "with leisure and good temper." His final barb, more stinging because it contained some truth, was unlikely to promote the desired "good temper." "Gentlemen now feel the weather warm," Gerry observed, "and the subject is warm, no wonder it produces some degree of heat; perhaps as our next will be a winter session, we may go thro' more coolly and dispassionately."[17]

Would further debate in the freer atmosphere of a committee of the whole prove a waste of time? House members were divided on this as on virtually everything else. Theodore Sedgwick was eager to find any means to silence not only Gerry but all those who proposed motions and then would "dwell long upon them in committee." But John Page declared that a rush to end the discussion was an admission that the amendments were merely a "tub to a whale," unworthy of serious consideration.[18] Aedanus Burke of South Carolina agreed with the Virginian. Speaking as a champion of the people's liberties, he warned that cutting off the debate would send a clear and negative message to citizens everywhere. The people, Burke declared, knew that they had parted with their liberties when they ratified the Constitution. They had done so only with the hope that they would soon get those liberties back.

In the beginning, Madison's colleagues had considered a discussion of his proposals a waste of time; now, men on both sides of the aisle insisted that his amendments were too important a matter to hurry. In the face of pressure from both Federalists and Antifederalists, Fisher Ames withdrew his motion. And with that, the day's discussion ended. The House then resolved itself once more into a committee of the whole, this time to continue the debate over the several bills dealing with the establishment of the judicial system, the protection of congressional acts and records, and the promotion of science and useful arts.

That evening, South Carolina's William Smith recapped the day's heated arguments for Edward Rutledge. Not surprisingly, Smith, a Federalist, laid the blame for the discord squarely on the Antifederalists: "It is worthy of observation that the antifederals in our House have thrown difficulties in the way of these Amendmts. merely because they can't carry alterations which wod. overturn the Governmt." With obvious regret, he added that "there has been more ill-humour & rudeness displayed to day than has existed since the meeting of Congress—allowing to Gerry & one or two more—& to make it worse, the weather is intensely hot."[19]

IX

———

On Monday, August 17, the House began its day's deliberations with further discussion of the bill to promote the progress of science and useful arts. Then, it again configured itself as a committee of the whole to discuss amendments. There was no attempt to hide the fact that tempers were noticeably frayed and civility had worn thin. Like William Smith, most Federalists laid the blame on "Gerry Tucker &c" who, even outsiders believed, "appear determined to obstruct & embarrass the Business as much as possible."[1]

In this uncomfortable atmosphere, the committee took up the remaining guarantees grouped within the fourth proposal. Any hopes of amity or of a speedy vote flew out the window as soon as the first of these guarantees was presented. The proposal read: "A well regulated militia, composed of the body of the people, being the best security of a free state; the right of the people to keep and bear arms shall not be infringed, but no person, religiously scrupulous, shall be compelled to bear arms."[2]

At issue here was this: what restrictions, if any, should be placed on the composition of state-organized militias and what level of government—federal or state—was entitled to deploy these militias? To men like Elbridge Gerry, it was critical that the states maintain sole control of their militias, for these state armies were the last line of defense against a central government that might use its own military force, or call on cooperative state militias, to impose its will on sovereign states.

Gerry led off the discussion with an impassioned attack on the religious exemptions clause and the failure of the proposal to prevent the creation of a standing army. Great danger, he insisted, lay in the federal government's right to decide which religious denominations were exempt from military service. By the simple act of declaring a substantial number of faiths exempt, an abusive government could thin the ranks of men able to bear arms against it. Equally troubling to Gerry was the fact that the proposal did nothing to prevent the "bane of liberty," a standing army. All Congress had to do was transform state militias into such an army—and use it to oppress the people.

Gerry's argument left his colleagues amazed and bewildered. Many representatives found it based on tortured logic and improbable scenarios. Maryland Federalist Joshua Seney felt compelled to ask bluntly what Gerry could possibly be talking about. Gerry replied that the exemption from service should be given only to specifically designated religious sects. But his purpose eluded James Jackson, whose response indicated clearly that he did not share Gerry's fear of an abuse of military forces by the federal government. In an attempt to understand what so disturbed Gerry, Jackson asked: Was he concerned that the proposal contained a loophole that would allow men to avoid military service? Or perhaps Mr. Gerry supposed that all the men in America would become Quakers or Moravians to avoid defending their country from invasion? To remedy this sort of evasion of service, Jackson proposed instead that any man refusing to bear arms for religious scruples should be required to pay a fixed sum. William Smith of South Carolina then suggested that finding a substitute to serve ought to be an option as well.

As usual, Roger Sherman tried to interject some common sense and focus into the conversation. Wasn't it likely, he asked, that a man who had religious scruples against bearing arms would also have scruples against finding a substitute or paying for the privilege of his pacifism? And if a sect was specifically exempted from service, would this mean that any of its members who wished to bear arms would be refused? Unlike Jackson, Sherman grasped the nature of Gerry's complaint. But he dismissed as utter nonsense this fear that the federal government would create a standing army out of militias. The states, he reminded his colleagues, governed their militias.

If Sherman hoped the debate would end there, he was destined to be disappointed. The discussion dragged on, although most of the comments centered on rewording the proposition without significantly changing its terms or its intent. Only one representative, New York's Egbert Benson, challenged the proposition that "religious scruples" should serve as a basis for exemption. Pacifism might be a religious tenet for some, he said, but it was not a natural right. In the end, despite Gerry's dire warnings, Benson's objections, and all the proposed edits, the committee of the whole voted to approve the original proposal.

The committee moved on to the next guarantee under the umbrella of the fourth proposal. It read: "No soldier shall in time of peace be quartered in any house without the consent of the owner, nor in time of war, but in a manner to be prescribed by law." In a legislative body filled with revolutionary war veterans, signers of the Declaration of Independence, and patriots with long memories of British occupation and abuses, this guarantee against reviving one of the most hated practices of their colonial past was quickly approved.[3]

The next, or fifth, clause now came under consideration. It protected a person from being subjected to more than one trial or one punishment for the same offense, except in cases of impeachment. It secured the right of a person to refuse self-incrimination and ensured that no one could be deprived of life, liberty, or property without due process of law. Although none of the state ratifying conventions had demanded that private property could not be taken for public use without just compensation, Madison had included this guarantee in the list dealing with legal abuses.

Two of the many lawyers in the House, Egbert Benson and Roger Sherman, pointed out a flaw in the clause's phrasing. The intention was surely not to prevent a man from asking for a second trial if he was convicted but rather to prevent an acquitted man from being tried again. Benson felt this intention was unclear, but the House members decided to let the language stand. New York's John Laurance proved more persuasive on the issue of self-incrimination. He proposed that the right of an accused person to refuse to testify should apply only in criminal cases. The representatives agreed, and the fifth clause passed with little further discussion.[4]

The sixth clause—"Excessive bail shall not be required, nor excessive fines imposed, nor cruel and unusual punishments inflicted"—prompted a protracted meditation on the part of New Hampshire's Samuel Livermore. There seems to be much humanity in this clause, the usually reticent Livermore conceded, yet on reflection, he found it meaningless. What, after all, did excessive bail mean? Who would decide if the bail was reasonable or excessive? And as for cruel and unusual punishment, Livermore contended that "it is sometimes necessary to hang a man, villains often deserve whipping, and perhaps having their ears cut off." In Livermore's view, the prevention of vice must be among government's paramount concerns and, in the absence of effective lenient means to do so, the existing harsher means must not be set aside. Despite Livermore's defense of hanging, whipping, and dismemberment, the committee approved the clause with little additional debate.[5]

Most of the legislators seemed pleased with the pace they were setting, but Elbridge Gerry was not. In a less than subtle criticism of his colleagues, he announced his refusal to be rushed. He intended, he said, to read every word and clause of the committee's proposals with great care. Thus, when the seventh clause was presented, the sharp-eyed Gerry drew attention to a grammatical error. The offending clause read "the right of the people to be *secured* in their persons, houses, papers and effects, shall not be violated by warrants issued without probable cause." Gerry pointed out that the word "secured"—which meant kept safely—ought instead to be "secure," which meant enjoying a feeling of safety. Gerry's proposed correction, surprisingly terse and to the point, was accepted and the change was made.

The eighth clause was, in effect, the assurance clause that the inclusion of specific rights and liberties in these proposed amendments did not "deny or disparage others retained by the people." Once again Gerry decided to comment on the language. "Deny and disparage," he observed, was too vague; he moved that it be amended to read "deny or impair." And once again, the House committee members accepted his suggestion. And with that, the long list of rights guaranteed by proposal four was completed.

Madison was heavily invested in the next proposal. It guaranteed the equal right of conscience, freedom of the press, and trial by jury. The rights themselves were uncontroversial, but the umbrella extended to protect them was certain to be challenged. The proposal denied the state governments as well as the federal government any power to violate these rights.

Antifederalist members of the House recognized this for what it was: a challenge to the sovereign authority of the states. South Carolina's Thomas Tudor Tucker spoke for them when he declared it best "to leave the state governments to themselves, and not to interfere with them more than we already do." Many of us, he added, thought federal interference "rather too much" as it was. He demanded that this infraction of state sovereignty be deleted.[6]

Madison responded quickly. He personally believed this proposal, as worded, was the most important amendment of all. These rights, he argued, deserved protection from all levels of government, federal and state.

Madison was prepared for a long argument, but on this issue the Federalists were united; they asserted their power as a majority and quickly squelched Tucker's motion. The committee of the whole did, however, accept Samuel Livermore's suggestion that the negative phrasing of the clause be transformed into a positive statement: "The equal rights of conscience, the freedom of speech, or of the press, and the right of trial by jury in criminal cases shall not be infringed by any state."

The committee then dispatched the sixth proposition by defeating a motion to raise the threshold for appeals to the court from $1,000 to $3,000. That decided, they moved on to the seventh proposal, which would replace the third clause of the original Constitution, and which set down the procedures for trying crimes other than impeachment or military cases. The Federalist majority was united in support of this amendment, and this unanimity left little room for the success of even the mildest Antifederalist revisions.

It had become clear to Antifederalists that opposition was futile whenever the Federalist majority was united. Aedanus Burke, whose own modest motion—that the accused be allowed to put off his trial until the next court session—had just gone down to defeat, chose this moment to vent the frustration felt by the minority. "He was not much discouraged by the fate of his former motion," he declared with measured resignation. But he was determined to persist in the face of Federalist power. To prove his point, he promptly offered another motion. When it became obvious that this motion would suffer the same fate as his previous ones, he withdrew it. The Antifederalists had once again learned the hard lesson of majority rule.[7]

On Tuesday, August 18, the issue of amendments was the first item on the agenda. Elbridge Gerry had come prepared; he launched an attack on Madison and the select committee. He demanded once again that the committee of the whole consider not just the committee report but all the amendments proposed by the state ratifying conventions. He also proposed that any of these amendments ultimately accepted be placed on a par with those approved from the committee report. If Gerry's message had not been clear before, it was now: he suspected Madison's motives; he challenged the selections Madison had made from the more than two hundred proposals by the state conventions; and he condemned the Committee of Eleven's report as biased.

Gerry's motion prompted what the *Gazette* wryly described as "a warm debate." But the reporter from the *Congressional Register* noted that Thomas Tudor Tucker's speech, rather than Gerry's, aroused the ire of many Federalist members of the House.[8]

Tucker, who frequently insisted life was a "school for stoicism," demonstrated little of the Stoic when he spoke. He began by warning that a rejection of Gerry's motion would destroy the harmony that existed in the House. Many congressmen thought that this harmony was already gone, of course. But Tucker's next comments would do little to preserve or restore it. If the states were sufficiently chagrined at having their suggestions ignored, Tucker declared, they would turn to the only available remedy—a second convention. "The consequence of this may be disagreeable to the union," he said, for "party spirit may be revived, and animosities rekindled obstructive of tranquility." Indeed he was convinced that those animosities might be strong enough "to sever the union asunder."[9]

Warming to his subject, Tucker described a political Charybdis and Scylla: if a second convention is called, we may lose many of the "valuable principles" established by the Constitution; if a convention is not called, the government would be drastically weakened by a loss of the confidence and support of the people. "Which of the two evils is the greatest would be difficult to ascertain," he declared somberly.

Tucker struck a familiar chord: it was regrettable that amendments had not been passed before the Constitution was ratified. But the die was cast: the best possible course of action now must be to take up *all* the amendments that had been suggested. The House must consider each of them separately, and, after a candid and attentive debate, provide a vote of yea or nay on each of them. Although states might regret the rejection of some or any of their proposals, Tucker expressed hope that they would be "reconciled to this disappointment in consequence of such procedure." Having said his piece, Tucker announced he would not trespass further upon the patience of the House.

Madison, whose patience had certainly been trespassed upon, could muster only a mild attempt at peacemaking. He conceded that the amendments proposed by the states ought to be considered, but it would be "very inconvenient" to discuss them all at the present time. With that weak appeal for reasonableness, Madison left it to other Federalists to mount a more spirited opposition.

It fell to Jack Vining, a man given usually to florid metaphors and frequently bawdy speech, to make the simplest and most effective case against Gerry's motion. Since the House had already voted to refer the report of the Committee of Eleven to a committee of the whole, Vining noted, Gerry's motion was out of order. After brief discussion, the Federalists, firmly united, sent Gerry's motion down to defeat. Then, as if no challenge had been made, they turned their attention to the second clause of the seventh proposal, which they quickly and favorably dispatched.

The eighth proposal had only one purpose, but it was an important one: to reassure the people that the government would adhere to a strict separation of powers. None of the three branches of government, it declared, would trespass on the designated duties of the others. Roger Sherman, who had emerged as the minimalist among the Federalist representatives, objected that the amendment was altogether unnecessary. But Madison insisted it would bolster confidence in the new government. When the motion was put, it passed.

With that, the committee came, at last, to the final proposal. It spelled out the distribution of authority and power that defined the federal system:

"The powers not delegated by the constitution, nor prohibited by it to the states, are reserved to the states respectively." Yet as the debate began, it became clear that this distribution was not spelled out emphatically enough for the Antifederalist minority. Thomas Tudor Tucker called for the word "expressly" to be added so that the proposal would read "The powers not *expressly* delegated by this constitution . . ." A simple adverb could thus obliterate the "necessary and proper" clause of the Constitution.[10]

Although Tucker's motion was certain to go down to defeat, Madison decided to speak against it. It was "impossible to confine a government to the exercise of express powers," he insisted, "unless the constitution descended to recount every minutiae." Even the most ardent Antifederalists in the Virginia ratifying convention, he added, had not pressed a demand to limit the federal government to expressed powers only. There was little else to be said, for the Federalist majority had no intention of abandoning the necessary and proper clause. The proposal was approved as written.[11]

The discussion of the committee's report was nearing its end. The next step would be a formal vote by the House on what amounted to its own report to itself.[12]

Before the day ended, postmortems had begun to fill the representatives' correspondence. William Smith recounted to his son-in-law, Otho Holland Williams of Maryland, that civility had degenerated into "bad temper" after five days of protracted debate on the amendments. Federalists like Smith laid the blame squarely on the Antifederalist minority, which they described as willfully obstructionist. In a letter to Dr. Benjamin Rush, Pennsylvania's Frederick Muhlenberg summed up what he considered to be the ironies, absurdities, and hidden motives in the struggle between Federalists and Antifederalists. "It is a strange yet certain Fact," he observed, "that those who have heretofore been & still profess to be the greatest Sticklers for Amendments to the Constitution of the U.S. have hitherto thrown every Obstacle they could in their way & by lengthy Debates & numberless Amendts. Which they know full well neither 2/3ds of Congress nor 3 fourth of the different Legislatures would ever adopt, have endeavored to mar their progress, but it is obvious their Design was to favour their darling Question for calling a Convention." [13]

James Madison could have found both solace and vindication had he read Muhlenberg's analysis of the Antifederalist endgame. Noah Webster might have been right that Madison had not taken the pulse of the people accurately, but Madison's fears that Antifederalist leaders still yearned for a second convention seemed correct. Men like Smith and Muhlenberg certainly thought so. For his part, Madison remained convinced that he had read the Antifederalists' agenda properly—and had taken the necessary defensive steps to thwart them. Writing to his friend and sometime humorous critic, the Pennsylvania lawyer Richard Peters, Madison defended his decision to introduce the amendments. "If amendts. had not been proposed from the federal side of the House, the proposition would have come *within three days*, from the adverse side. It is certainly best that they appear to be the free gift of the friends of the Constitution rather than extorted by the address & weight of its enemies." Madison was more confident than ever before that his strategy would prevent the people from rallying if and when the Antifederalists chose to "blow the Trumpet for a second Convention." [14]

X

―――――

On Wednesday, August 19, the House met to consider the report it had just completed as a committee of the whole. By that time, the heat wave was in its second week and, according to George Clymer, it had caused several fatalities. In a House dominated by Federalists, there was little doubt that the report would meet the two-thirds vote required for adoption. Still, as this was likely to be the last opportunity to press for changes, everyone expected—or feared—another lengthy debate.[1]

The discussion began, not with Antifederalists on the attack, but with the airing of a familiar disagreement among the Federalists. Roger Sherman, who had never accepted the plan to integrate the amendments into the body of the original Constitution, now moved for the third time that they be added instead as a supplement. Unlike some of his Federalist colleagues, Sherman did not consider it sacrilege to tamper with the original text. Yet he did believe that inserting changes infringed on the people's will. He conceded that Elbridge Gerry was correct: the voters had not elected the delegates to the Philadelphia convention. However, in Sherman's view Gerry had missed the point. The delegates had written the Constitution in the name of the American people, and their handiwork was ratified by popularly elected conventions.

Sherman had made this argument before, of course, but this time he added a warning. The fate of the amendments rested in the hands of state governments. Not only were these governments capable of acting against the wishes of their citizens; they were also capable of tampering in unpredictable ways with the powers already granted in the Constitution. Sherman urged his fellow Federalists to be wary of offering any opening for a renewed discussion of the original text.

The debate over Sherman's motion—sandwiched as it was between a few petitions to the House and a discussion of the Senate's version of a judiciary bill—occupied the entire session on amendments. In the end, his warning that putting them into the original text was risky had the desired effect. When the vote came, two thirds of the House supported his motion.[2]

The press coverage of the day's debate on amendments was sparse, perhaps an indication of the public's waning interest in this particular political issue. It seemed obvious that the Federalists were in firm control of the presidency, the Senate, and the House, and their decision to add a bill of rights to the Constitution could only cement their dominance. The *Congressional Register*, which would eventually become the *Congressional Record*, characterized the debate as a "desultory conversation" and devoted only a few paragraphs to the House discussion. The issue of amendments was no longer front-page news.[3]

That evening, Madison wrote a long letter to Richard Peters, justifying his decision to undertake what Peters had, in jest, referred to as "the nauseous project of amendments." Why, on the brink of success, Madison felt it necessary to defend his actions is unclear. Perhaps one of his final comments holds a clue: "In Virga. a majority of the Legislature last elected, is bitterly opposed to the Govt. and will be joined, if no amends. be proposed, by great nos. of the other side who will complain of being deceived." This continuing concern about the loyalties of Virginians was revealing; James Madison's nationalism had not entirely triumphed over his identification with the place of his birth.[4]

The discussion of the amendments report resumed on Thursday, August 20. Sherman's success in overturning the committee's original decision had clearly encouraged several House members to press for other reversals. According to the *Gazette of the United States,* the second proposed amendment was met with a host of new propositions and motions relating to the optimal number of representatives in the House. All of these failed to find traction and were tabled.

The next discussion, on militia service, prompted a reprise of the disjointed and often outlandish debate over the right to refuse service on religious grounds. This time, Thomas Scott of Pennsylvania proved more radical than Elbridge Gerry. Gerry had proposed only that sects to be exempted should be specified. Scott warned against any religious exemptions at all. The scenario he presented was both novel and decidedly extreme. Religion, he explained, was rapidly declining and soon there would be no genuine faith at all. When that day came, the nation's many "freethinkers" would have no compunction about pretending to be Moravians or Quakers in order to avoid military service. Apparently none of Scott's colleagues shared this dark vision of faithless cowards ready to feign pacifism. After a few unrelated comments, the committee's language on the subject was adopted.[5]

On the third day of House discussion, the Antifederalists reentered the debate, and the heated arguments everyone had expected began. The acrimonious exchanges that followed dramatized the difference between the two parties' perception of what dangers lay ahead for the republic. These exchanges also made clear the unassailable power of the Federalists when they were united.

The Antifederalists proved ready to make a final quixotic attempt to restrict the powers of the federal government. If nothing else, their motions, taken together, would constitute a ringing statement of their belief that the greatest dangers lay in a strong central government. Elbridge Gerry, who had emerged as the leading champion of states' rights, began by proposing once again that "expressly" be inserted into the ninth amendment. The goal was, as it had been from the beginning, to limit the federal government only to those powers explicitly stated in the Constitution. The addition of "expressly" would prevent the government from extending its reach through the necessary and proper clause. Gerry insisted that this proposed change was so important that the ayes and noes ought to be taken. The House complied but the motion failed.[6]

It came as no surprise when Gerry's motion was defeated. But its failure prompted the South Carolinian Aedanus Burke to address the House. Burke articulated his party's determination to stand its ground and fight for its principles, even in the face of certain defeat. "The majority of this House may be inclined to think all our propositions unimportant," he said, but we do not. To demonstrate that he, like Gerry, would continue to challenge the erosion of state sovereignty, Burke immediately moved for a limitation on the federal government's role in the election of members of Congress. "I move you, sir," Burke said, addressing the chair of the House, "to add to the articles of amendment, the following, 'Congress shall not alter, modify, or interfere in the times, places, or manner of holding elections of senators, or representatives, except when any state shall refuse or neglect, or be unable, by invasion or rebellion, to make such election.'"[7]

Fisher Ames, unmoved by Burke's frustration or by his dedication to the Antifederalist cause, offered the majority party's response to the motion. The power of Congress to adjust the rules governing election of its members was essential; it was the only way to prevent "improper regulations, calculated to answer party purposes only." Ames did not have to offer the most egregious examples of party purposes, since the delaying tactics of New Jersey and New York in both electing and appointing members to this first session of Congress were fresh in everyone's memory.

Madison decided to join the discussion with a blunt and unsympathetic comment on the futility of the Antifederalists' resistance. There was no point, he declared with obvious impatience, in proposing changes to the committee report when those changes had no chance of passage. But rather than ending the conflict, Madison's statement of the obvious added fuel to the Antifederalists' fire.

To no one's surprise, Elbridge Gerry refused to let the matter drop. What motive, he asked, did the Congress have for insisting on a power certain to be "so obnoxious to almost every state?" To Gerry, the answer was clear: congressional control over the election of its members was part of a Federalist plan to "establish a government of an arbitrary kind." The Federalists' endgame was tyranny and their strategy was intimidation and placing hurdles in the way of the exercise of voting rights: first, the government would require every person to publicly announce his vote, subjecting ordinary citizens to pressures by their social betters; next it would order elections to be held at remote places where only the friends of government-favored candidates could attend. Was this likely to happen? Gerry, for one, was certain it would. And when it did, he declared, there would be a "Farewell to the rights of the people, even to elect their own representatives." [8]

Maryland's Michael Jenifer Stone rejected Gerry's dark scenario; yet, as a defender of state sovereignty, he was ready to support Burke's motion. But when William Loughton Smith of South Carolina attempted to win additional support for the motion, he unwittingly sidetracked the entire debate. Smith claimed that eight states had expressed a desire to see congressional power over elections limited to emergencies. But as soon as he named the states—New Hampshire, Massachusetts, New York, Pennsylvania, Maryland, Virginia, North Carolina, and South Carolina—he was challenged. Maryland had done no such thing, declared Daniel Carroll. Pennsylvania's Thomas Fitzsimons also denied that his state had raised this issue. Smith refused to back down, insisting that Maryland's convention had included this amendment among those it had submitted to Congress, but Maryland's Stone, like Carroll, denied it. In the end, Smith was forced to admit he did not actually know how these state declarations "came into the world." He could only insist, somewhat lamely, that he had certainly seen them somewhere.

At this point, Theodore Sedgwick stepped in with a compromise resolution. He proposed that the Congress have the power to alter the times, manner, and places of holding elections *only if* the states specified improper ones and thus abused their powers. This proposal satisfied neither Federalists nor Antifederalists, and the verbal sparring began anew with a frustrated Thomas Tudor Tucker taking up the banner of states' rights once more.

It was Tucker's wish "that the state legislatures might be left to themselves to perform every thing they were competent to do, without the guidance of congress." To this, Benjamin Goodhue countered with typical nationalist sentiment. His greatest apprehension was not any federal plot against the states, but that the state governments would "oppose and thwart the general one to such a degree as finally to overturn it." The exchange captured the most basic difference of perception between Federalists and Antifederalists. Tucker and his fellow Antifederalists saw a plot by an unrestrained federal government to steadily reduce the power and autonomy of the states. Goodhue and his party saw a struggling federal government, defending itself against the still more powerful states. As long as the states had the upper hand, men like Goodhue and Ames and Madison were convinced the federal government must have every power necessary for its self-preservation. Goodhue had set down his view of the relative powers of the federal and state governments in a letter to a Massachusetts merchant, Michael Hodge. The truth, he declared, "is, that so far from the State Governments being in hazard from the National Government, the danger is wholy on the other side."[9]

After the exchange between Tucker and Goodhue, Aedanus Burke rose to speak. Burke had a reputation for believing in political conspiracies, and he had long feared that plots to create an American aristocracy would destroy the country's hard-won republicanism. In 1783, he had written a widely distributed pamphlet attacking the formation of the Society of the Cincinnati, an organization of former Continental Army officers and their French counterparts who were veterans of the American Revolution. The society—which boasted that Henry Knox, Nathanael Greene, Alexander McDougall, and George Washington were among its founding members—had been created to promote patriotism, to foster fellowship among its members, and to provide assistance to members or their widows and children in times of need. But Burke sincerely believed its restriction of membership to these veterans and their male descendants cleared the way for a permanent aristocracy. This defining suspicion that republicanism was under attack—by the Society of the Cincinnati, by British merchants, and by Federalists—had made the ever-vigilant Burke an opponent of ratification and, in Congress, an opponent of everything from a standing army to the creation of federal district courts. Thus his despair was both genuine and palpable as he warned of the dangers of federal control of congressional elections.[10]

This effort by Burke to curtail federal power, like many other measures proposed by him and by Tucker and Gerry, was destined to go down to defeat—and Burke clearly knew it. Rather than continue the argument, he chose to deliver a brief, mournful speech, laying out the Antifederalist mission. Americans who ratified the Constitution without calling for any prior amendments did so, he declared, out of patriotism. They had parted with their liberties believing that Congress would restore these—and this was what he and his fellow Antifederalists were trying, but failing, to ensure would be done.[11]

The House now moved on to a debate that the Congressional Register again characterized as a "desultory," over the ultimate number of representatives to make up the House. After agreeing to raise the upper limit to two hundred, the weary representatives ended their consideration of amendments for the day and turned, no doubt with relief, to a discussion of the Senate bill on establishing the judicial courts of the United States.

On Saturday, August 22, the Antifederalists mounted their final, and boldest, effort to curtail the powers of the federal government. Perhaps they felt they had nothing to lose by a frontal attack on the Constitution, since both this first House session and the debate over the amendments were coming to an end. They took aim against the most fundamental power of any government: the power to tax. Thomas Tudor Tucker led the way with a motion that the *Congressional Register* reported as: "Congress shall never impose direct taxes but where the monies arising from the duties, imposts and excise are insufficient for the public exigencies, nor then until congress shall have made a requisition upon the states to assess, levy, and pay their respective proportions of such requisitions. And in case any state shall neglect, or refuse to pay its proportion, pursuant to such requisition, then congress may assess, and levy such states proportioned, together with the interest thereon at the rate of 6 per cent, per annum, from the time of payment prescribed by such requisition." The *Gazette of the United States,* a newspaper openly sympathetic to the Federalists, offered its readers a simpler, bare-bones version: "That Congress shall not exercise the power of levying direct taxes, except in cases where any of the States shall refuse, or neglect to comply with their requisitions." But readers of both the *Register* and the *Gazette* knew that Tucker was proposing a return to a dependence on requisitions that had failed so dismally to sustain the Confederation.[12]

John Page, throwing his support to the Federalist position, attempted to quash the motion on procedural grounds: the issue at hand was the report by the committee of the whole, and the introduction of a completely new amendment was out of order. Tucker, however, refused to withdraw his proposal, arguing that the proposition had been referred to the select committee but that this committee had declined to report on it. This, he said, gave him the right to have it discussed and voted on now.

Tucker's insistence forced the pro-government majority to respond to the content of the motion. James Jackson of Georgia, whose fiery temperament had embroiled him in a number of duels and street brawls, was the first to take up the fight. He began by reminding his colleagues of the disastrous effects of the Confederation's reliance on requisitions. Then, warming to his subject, he spelled out what he believed would be the dire consequences if Tucker's proposal was accepted. A requisition system would excite jealousy among the states and lead to insurrections, if not to a civil war. The union would thus dissolve, the republic would be exposed to the contempt of foreign nations, and invasion by a European power would quickly follow. Put in less dramatic terms, without the right of taxation, the federal government could not honor its debts, maintain domestic law and order, or protect its borders.

After several additional comments, Elbridge Gerry suggested that the proposal be sent to another select committee. Then, ignoring his own suggestion almost immediately, Gerry launched into a spirited attack on the government's taxing powers, producing yet another of his dark scenarios: the federal power to tax would annihilate the state governments or, failing that, it would force double taxation on individual citizens. "What umbrage must it give every individual," he declared, "to have two setts of collectors and tax-gathers surrounding their doors." Here he was taking a page from Patrick Henry's book, for this theme of double tax collectors at the door had been a favorite of Henry's during the Virginia ratification debates.[13]

In the end, no argument the Antifederalists mustered could overcome the political reality that Federalists dominated the proceedings in the House. When the vote was taken, the Tucker amendment went down to defeat. The long process that began with James Madison's proposal of amendments on May 4 was finally over. The next hurdle was the Senate.

XI

———

On August 23, Benjamin Goodhue wrote to friends in Salem, Massachusetts. "We have at last so far got through the wearisome business of amendments to the great joy of I believe every member of the House." He was clearly relieved that there was "nothing . . . left but for a committee so to put the amendments in order that they may stand properly arranged."

Goodhue, like most of his colleagues, regretted the time spent on an issue less pressing than raising revenue. But the amendment debates had cost the House more than time taken from more serious issues; it had silenced the claims of goodwill and harmony that had appeared in congressional correspondence in May and June. Indeed, by the end of the process in the House, the anger and frustration had grown so intense that two duels were only narrowly avoided. The first of these incidents involved Aedanus Burke and Fisher Ames; the second, Elbridge Gerry and an unknown member of the House. In an era when honor and reputation were of paramount importance to political leaders, men often barely escaped the dueling fields. But during the debate over the amendments, both the irascible Gerry and the mournfully sincere Burke had felt provoked enough to invoke the code duello.[1]

Goodhue blamed the Antifederalists for dragging out the debates over amendments. From his perspective, the House minority had been intentionally obstructionist: "Those who were not friendly to the Constitution made every effort with their most persevering diligence to introduce a variety of propositions which a large majority of the House deemed totally inadmissible." He was convinced that, in the end, the Antifederalists were not so discontented as they pretended to be. "[A]t length after exhausting themselves as well as the patience of their brethren," he observed, "they appear tolerably satisfied with the issue of the business." As for him, he hoped the matter was finally settled and "we may never hear any more of it."[2]

Goodhue offered no criticism of James Madison, the man responsible for raising "the business" in the first place. Yet there were others who doubted Madison's wisdom in proposing the amendments. Philadelphia's Robert Morris believed it had all been for naught. He did not expect "the Nonesense they call Amendments" to survive in the Senate or to win approval by the requisite number of state legislatures.[3]

Did Morris's sentiments bode ill for the fate of the amendments in the Senate? Certainly the Senate, like the House, was a Federalist stronghold. No matter what their politics, however, the men of the Senate, like those of the House, were drawn from America's elite. Of the twenty-two senators in 1789, over half were college educated in the United States or abroad. Although several, such as William Few of Georgia and Richard Bassett of Delaware, began life in humble circumstances, far more had been born to wealth and privilege. Over half were lawyers and, again like the members of the House, most were veterans of the Revolutionary War. Almost half of the senators—including Connecticut's two members, William Samuel Johnson and Oliver Ellsworth, Delaware's George Read and Richard Bassett, and William Paterson of New Jersey—had played a role in drafting the Constitution, and at least sixteen had served in the Continental and Confederation Congresses. The great majority shared a political as well as a social profile: only four members could be consistently found in the Antifederalist camp. Thus, here as in the House, Antifederalists would be out-voted if they proposed restraints on the Constitution's powers.[4]

Benjamin Goodhue had predicted that the Senate would delay any consideration of the amendments until the next session. But the senators decided to take them up in early September. Their discussions, unlike those of the House, were conducted without the press or observers in the galleries, for the senators had refused to make their sessions public. It is difficult to know what tensions, if any, developed in their discussions, therefore, or to gauge whether the debates turned acrimonious or remained civil. One of the few windows into the workings of the Senate during the summer and fall of 1789 comes from the daily diary kept by William Maclay of Pennsylvania. It is doubtful that his reporting was unbiased, for the very democratic Maclay disliked many of the senators he considered aristocratic. His personal disdain for them is evident in the diary pages. Here, he declared Connecticut's Oliver Ellsworth so verbose that "I think he may well be styled the 'Endless Ellsworth.'" He also damned Ellsworth as a man without "a particle of integrity"; then, not content to criticize an individual, Maclay decided to damn the man's entire state. "Perhaps such a quality [as integrity] is useless in Connecticut." He had an equally low opinion of the Virginia senators, whom he found tiresome in their admiration of the president: "No Virginian," he wrote, "can talk on any subject, but the perfection of General Washington interweaves itself into every conversation." He was vitriolic when it came to New Yorkers: "These Yorkers are the vilest of people. Their vices resemble bad schoolboys who are unfortunate at play: they revenge themselves by telling enormous thumpers." Maclay was equally uncharitable toward the Senate's presiding officer, Vice President John Adams, whom he intensely disliked. He ridiculed Adams's fondness for pomp and circumstance. Adams clearly returned the antipathy, for he declared Maclay a dullard.[5]

Maclay's entry of August 25 reflected his typical mixing of political insight with personal prejudice: "The amendments to the Constitution sent from the House of Representatives. They were treated contemptuously by Izard, Langdon and Mr. Morris. Izard moved that they should be postponed to next Session. Langdon seconded & Mr. Morris got up and spoke angrily but not well. They however lost their Motion and Monday was assigned for the taking them up."[6]

Unfortunately on September 2, the day the debate on the amendments began in earnest, Maclay was in bed, nursing what he called an "acute pain in his loins." He remained absent from the Senate throughout the debates, although he continued to enter daily accounts in his diary of the news brought to him by colleagues and friendly visitors. It is telling that he makes no further mention of the amendments; if the entries made in the diary during his illness are a fair barometer, the Senate was far more interested in the issue of a permanent location for the federal government and far more invested in setting generous salaries for senators.[7]

It took only a week for the Senate to finish its work on the amendments. The version it forwarded to the House contained twelve amendments, the result of some condensation and some elimination of proposals in the House version. The senators collapsed into one the House's Article 3, prohibiting Congress from establishing a national religion or interfering with the free exercise of a religion; and Article 4, which covered freedom of speech, the press, assembly, and petition. After amending Article 11 several times, the Senate decided to merge House Articles 10 and 11, both of which covered procedures for trials, the former for criminal trials and the latter for civil trials. These condensations required the renumbering of the articles.[8]

Occasionally, a Senate revision of language altered the content of an amendment. For example, the wordy tenth amendment in the House version was revised to read simply "No person shall be held to answer for a capital, or otherwise infamous crime, unless on presentment or indictment by a Grand Jury." Lost in the revision was the guarantee that a man would be tried in his own vicinage or community. This omission was likely to prompt protest when the Senate version reached the House. In a letter to Samuel Phillips of Massachusetts, Benjamin Goodhue called the "vicinage" clause "the darling object with the Virginians who have been the great movers in amendments." In the final version produced by a joint committee of the two chambers, the right to a trial in one's locality was restored through the phrase "an impartial jury of the State and district wherein the crime shall have been committed."[9]

The Senate did make substantive changes, small and large. In House Article 1, for example, the Senate chose to increase the number of persons per representative once the House reached two hundred from one per fifty thousand to one per sixty thousand. In the end it would not matter, for the states did not ratify this amendment.

In the Senate, as in the House, the Antifederalist minority attempted to restrict the federal government's power. According to Theodorick Bland Randolph, Senator Richard Henry Lee had hoped to "strike out the standing army in time of peace," but Lee "could not carry it." In a second significant effort, the Antifederalists moved to insert "to instruct their representatives" as one of the rights of the people in the now condensed Articles 3 and 4. The motion fared no better in the Senate than in the House; in both it was resoundingly defeated.[10]

Several abortive efforts by Federalist senators suggested that they trusted ordinary citizens far less than their counterparts in the House did. In Virginia, the Antifederalist Theodorick Bland Randolph was horrified when he learned from Senator Richard Henry Lee that there had been an attempt to eliminate the protection of speech and the press on the grounds that these freedoms "only tend to promote licenciousness." If such an effort had succeeded, he added, "god knows what will follow." Young John Randolph reported hearing of an equally terrifying restriction favored by the Senate. Writing to his stepfather, St. George Tucker, he declared that "a majority of the Senate were for not allowing the militia arms." Randolph believed the senators' motives were transparent: they were afraid that armed militias would put a stop to what he called the steady move to "Tyranny & Oppression." To Randolph's relief, this restriction could not muster the needed two-thirds vote.[11]

Perhaps the two most dramatic Senate changes centered on House Articles 14 and 17. The first was a crushing defeat for Madison-style nationalism; the second, a resounding victory. On September 7, the Senate completely eliminated the power of the federal government to prevent states from threatening their citizens' right of trial by jury in criminal cases or their freedom of conscience, speech, and the press. Because the senators depended for their seats on their state legislatures, few of them were eager to endorse the principle that the federal government could dictate specific policy to the states. Article 14 thus went down to defeat in the Senate. On the other hand, Federalists everywhere must have breathed a sigh of relief when the Senate blocked an effort to have "expressly" added to House Article 17, just as the House had done on two separate occasions.

Although Roger Sherman thought the Senate's work had improved the amendments, Antifederalists such as Elbridge Gerry and Senator Richard Henry Lee were appalled at the changes. Writing to his brother Francis Lightfoot Lee on September 13, Richard Henry Lee fumed: "They [the amendments] have at length passed the Senate, with difficulty, after being much mutilated and enfeebled—It is too much the fashion now to look at the Rights of the People, as a Miser inspects a Security, to find out a flaw." Lee despaired of the nation's future; "What with design in some, and fear of Anarchy in others, it is very clear, I think, that a government very different from a free one will take place e'er many years are passed."[12]

Gerry viewed the work of both houses of Congress with disdain. He told New York State senator John Wendell that the proposed amendments would do nothing to solve the central problems with the Constitution. Gerry understood that the purpose of Madison's bill of rights was to isolate the leadership of the Antifederalists from their broad base of followers— and he lamented the strategy's success. The only purpose these amendments would serve, he explained to Wendell, was "to reconcile those who had no adequate idea of the essential defects of the Constitution." He was satisfied, he hastened to add, that he had done all he could, both in the constitutional convention and in Congress, to avert the "injurious or ruinous" consequences of Federalist politics.[13]

Yet, despite the election and appointment of a Federalist majority in Congress, despite the defeat of most Antifederalist motions in both chambers, there were Antifederalists unwilling to abandon their struggle. These men continued to nurture the hope that, somehow, and at some point in the not too distant future, a sufficient number of states would rally to the call for a second convention. In a long and bitter letter to Patrick Henry, Richard Henry Lee acknowledged that all their attempts to make the amendments proposed by "our country" (by which he meant Virginia) had proved futile. As he put it: "We might as well have attempted to move Mount Atlas upon our shoulders." Nevertheless he continued to believe that soon enough other states would join in a demand for a new convention. These men may have been few, but to Madison they were proof he was correct: enemies of the new government remained—and they were remarkably tenacious.[14]

On September 14, the Senate sent its revised version of the amendments back to the House. Many in the House, especially those who yearned for this first session of Congress to end, feared that more debate lay ahead. As James Madison commented to Edmund Pendleton that day: "The difficulty of uniting the minds of men accustomed to think and act differently can only be conceived by those who have witnessed it."[15]

As members of the House steeled themselves against the likelihood of a new struggle, several believed the stumbling block to acceptance of the Senate version would be James Madison himself. On September 15, 1789, Congressman Fisher Ames warned Senator Caleb Strong that "many in our house, Mr. Madison, in particular, thinks, that they have lost much of their Sedative Virtue by the alteration." Given the acrimony produced by the ongoing battle over the location of the federal capital, the possibility of renewed fighting over the amendments filled Ames with dread. "A contest on this subject between the two houses would be very disagreeable," he told Strong.[16]

Ames had gauged Madison's mood well. New Hampshire senator Paine Wingate, a Federalist, echoed Ames when he wrote to Senator John Langdon that "Madison says he had rather have none than those agreed to by the Senate." Yet the fears these men expressed that Madison would dig in his heels proved unfounded. On September 21, Madison accepted appointment to a committee to confer with counterparts from the Senate. Together, he, Roger Sherman, and Jack Vining would be expected to negotiate with senators Oliver Ellsworth of Connecticut, Charles Carroll of Maryland, and William Paterson of New Jersey. As all six members of this conference committee were Federalists, there was little controversy. Within three days, the committee presented its report: the Senate version would stand, with only two exceptions.[17]

The first change to the Senate version was to have the third article read: "Congress shall make no law *respecting an establishment of Religion,* or prohibiting the free exercise thereof; or abridging the freedom of Speech, or of the Press, or the right of the people peaceably to assemble and to petition the Government for a redress of grievances." The second restored to what had become Article 8 the guarantee of a trial in the "district wherein the crime shall have been committed," and added several rights for the defendant. The accused was "to be informed of the nature and cause of the accusation; to be confronted with the witnesses against him; and to have compulsory process for obtaining Witnesses in his favour, & to have the assistance of counsel for his defence." Both of these revisions, to which the Senate members of the committee agreed, could be considered a victory for Madison and his fellow Virginians. The prohibition against the establishment of a national religion had been strengthened—something of great importance to James Madison, and, although the word "vicinage" was not restored in Article 8, a person accused of a crime would now be guaranteed a trial in a familiar setting.

On September 24, the House approved the committee's report with only six dissenters, all of them Antifederalists. Voting no were Theodorick Bland of Virginia, Elbridge Gerry of Massachusetts, Aedanus Burke, Thomas Tudor Tucker and Thomas Sumter of South Carolina, and John Page of Virginia. The next day, the Senate agreed to incorporate the House changes into the committee report. A week later, the president submitted Congress's handiwork to the states for ratification. By then, the weary House had adjourned.

Congress's role in creating a bill of rights had ended. The fate of these amendments now rested with the state legislatures. Yet many Antifederalists still smarted over the defeats they had been dealt in this first federal Congress. Virginians, in particular, had suffered blows to both their political agenda and their pride; they had failed to see genuine alterations made to the Constitution, and they had lost the first round of the battle over locating the federal capital in Pennsylvania. Their sense of loss was heightened by the knowledge that they had been outmaneuvered in both matters. Richard Henry Lee fumed to Patrick Henry about the farcical set of amendments the Federalists wanted ratified, asking "how wonderfully scrupulous have they been in stating Rights? The english language has been carefully culled to find words feeble in their Nature or doubtful their meaning!" [18]

William Grayson's anger was equally palpable. After lamenting to

Henry about the "disagreable altercations on the score of the seat of government," Grayson went on to declare that the Senate had destroyed even the appearance of protecting the people's rights. The Senate's betrayal of the people came as no surprise to him, however. "With respect to amendments matters have turned out exactly as I apprehended from the extrord[inar]y doctrine of playing the after game: the lower house sent up amendments which held out a safeguard to pers[on]al liberty in a great many instances, but this disgusted the Senate, and though we made every exertion to save them, they are so mutilated & gutted that in fact they are good for nothing." Despite all the defeats and setbacks endured during the first session of Congress, Grayson, like Richard Henry Lee, remained hopeful. "The Virginia amendments were all brought into view, and regular rejected," he wrote. Yet, "Perhaps they may think differently on the subject the next session." In the report that Grayson and Richard Henry Lee sent to Thomas Mathews, the speaker of the Virginia house of delegates, the same note of optimism was sounded: The antiadministration men predicted a second convention would soon be called.[19]

In the end, most Antifederalist veterans of the amendment battles had arrived at the same conclusion as Elbridge Gerry: the Bill of Rights was designed to be a distraction from a serious reevaluation of the Constitution. Thomas Tudor Tucker summed up the nature of Madison's victory: "You will find our Amendments to the Constitution calculated merely to amuse, or rather to deceive." In Tucker's view, the tub had indeed been tossed to the whale.[20]

XII

———

Congress officially adjourned on September 29 and members eagerly made their plans for returning home. Roger Sherman told his friend Simeon Baldwin he would head back to Connecticut that very week. On October 3, the *Providence Gazette* reported the arrival by ship of Benjamin Goodhue, who was headed eventually to Massachusetts, and Senator Paine Wingate, bound for Stratham, New Hampshire. Wingate's journey went well, but trouble struck soon after he arrived home. While he and his wife slept, a burglar entered their house and stole silver, one of the senator's overcoats, and a hat. Fortunately, the thief was captured.[1]

Elbridge Gerry was also the victim of theft. On his "disagreable & unfortunate" journey home his trunk, filled with private papers and correspondence, was stolen. Writing to his wife, Ann, who was still in New York, Gerry observed that "so many unhappy events in so short a period produced a depression of spirits" which he feared might wreck his health.[2]

For some, the journey home was more arduous than for others. George Thatcher was seriously ill by the time he arrived in Massachusetts. And James Madison, exhausted by his efforts in the first session of the Congress, was overtaken by sickness on his journey and had to pause in Philadelphia. He did not reach his home, Montpelier, until November 2. Here he waited to learn if his strategy would finally bear fruit: would the proposed Bill of

Rights splinter the Antifederalist coalition of leaders who sought structural changes to the Constitution and their followers who simply wanted their liberties protected? If so, ratification of the amendments would be ensured and the danger of a second convention would be finally, permanently laid to rest.[3]

Madison may have been anxious about the fate of his political strategy, but the French ambassador, the comte de Moustier, was certain of its effectiveness. In his summary of the first session of the American Congress, enclosed in a letter to the comte de Montmorin dated October 3, 1789, he observed: "The amendments that Congress proposed do not change any essential part; they serve rather as explication and corollary to this instrument, which is already considered with a kind of respect and which is no longer allowed to be touched without raising a clamor from patriots."[4]

Before the month was out, Madison received the welcome news that the first state had ratified the amendments. Once again a small state, this time New Jersey, had taken the lead. On November 20, its legislature agreed to eleven of the twelve amendments, voting nay only on the amendment dealing with congressional pay.[5]

On December 1, however, bad news arrived. Georgia had rejected all twelve amendments. Its legislature's decision revealed how unpredictable partisan politics could be. The rationale offered by Georgia Antifederalists was familiar to the Federalists who now stood solidly behind ratification of the Bill of Rights: it was premature, Georgia declared, to consider amendments before the new Constitution had an opportunity to be tested.

Better news came on December 19, for Maryland had ratified all twelve amendments. The news coming from North Carolina on December 22 was mixed. This state, which had finally joined the union in November 1789, ratified all of the amendments, but it instructed its congressional delegation to press for eight additional amendments. These amendments included limiting the power of Congress to regulate federal elections, a subject that had been thoroughly debated in the House. Another would require a severe limitation: a two-thirds vote in both the House and the Senate in order to pass any commercial legislation. Still, North Carolina was in the "yes" column and thus, as 1789 ended, three states had given their support to the Bill of Rights.[6]

On January 19, 1790, South Carolina also ratified it, but this state went further than North Carolina in seeking to secure additional amendments. South Carolina's congressmen were told to press for all the amendments their ratifying convention had proposed in 1788.

For Madison and for staunch Federalists everywhere South Carolina's demands for additional amendments must have been unsettling, because they included a limit on the power of Congress to levy direct taxes. This was exactly the kind of structural change Madison had labored so diligently to avoid.

On January 25, New Hampshire became the fifth state to ratify, although, like New Jersey, it refused to support the amendment on congressional salaries. The following day Delaware ratified all but the amendment that dealt with the number of representatives.

By February, four of the largest and most influential states—New York, Massachusetts, Virginia, and Pennsylvania—had still not made a decision on the amendments. In New York, once a stronghold of Antifederalism, political change worked in favor of Madison's handiwork. In the spring of 1789, Antis lost control of the state senate; they retained their control of the assembly but lost critical seats there as well. After considerable debate, New York became the seventh state to ratify the Bill of Rights, endorsing all but the amendment on the size of the House, which it defeated roundly by a vote of 52–5 on February 27. From the point of view of local Antifederalists, ratification of the amendments did not alter the fact that their state had given only qualified approval of the Constitution.[7]

The politics of Massachusetts proved far more complex—and with Elbridge Gerry on the scene, far more dramatic. As the Antifederalist Jeremiah, Gerry warned that both excise taxes and direct taxes loomed on the horizon if structural changes were not made to the Constitution. But in January 1790, former Antifederalist governor John Hancock sent a message to his legislature urging ratification of the proposed amendments. The state senate complied, approving all but the first and second. The state senators then called for a joint committee of senate and assembly to ensure agreement between the two bodies. The assembly members of this committee agreed to strike amendments one and two, but also demanded that a third amendment be rejected. They could not endorse the proposal establishing the distribution of powers between federal and state governments, they said, on the grounds that it did not contain the limiting word "expressly." The senate members concurred, and a second joint committee was then appointed to bring in the state's bill of ratification. But somehow and for some reason lost to history, no such bill was ever officially issued. In fact, along with Georgia and Connecticut, Massachusetts did not formally ratify the Bill of Rights until 1939. Meanwhile a third committee was formed to recommend additional amendments. Its members declared their desire to preserve what they called a "federal republic." Thus it was not surprising that among their recommendations were several familiar Antifederalist demands. These included the restriction on any interference in federal elections unless a state refused to hold them, a prohibition on grants of commercial monopolies, and the defining effort to restrict the federal government, the addition of "expressly" to the powers amendment. Federalists saw this committee's work as a blatant attempt to strengthen Antifederalist sentiment in neighboring Rhode Island, the last remaining holdout from the union.[8]

On March 10 Pennsylvania joined the "yes" column, rejecting only the first and second proposed amendments. Pennsylvania's ratification was a welcome victory for the Federalists, since the state had strong Antifederalist sentiments and there were several influential members of the opposition in the state government. A newspaper campaign against ratification had begun even before the final congresssional approval of the twelve amendments. Philadelphia's *Independent Gazetteer* had carried a strong attack on the Bill of Rights by an Antifederal essayist thought to be Samuel Bryan. Bryan, reprising his role as "Centinel" on September 9, 1789, warned his fellow Pennsylvanians that they were being duped; "many of these amendments are very proper and necessary," he wrote, but as long as no amendments significantly restricted the powers of the new government, they were nothing more than "an insult upon the understanding and discernment of the people." Congress, he declared, filled as it was with "votaries of ambition," had shown its true colors when it refused to limit the government's powers by adding "expressly" to its twelfth amendment. Centinel's final condemnation was ringing: "If Machiavel were to rise from the dead, he would be lost in admiration, at the prodigious improvements made upon his code of disingenuous and deceptive policy." Despite such stinging criticism, Pennsylvania's legislature had voted yes to ten of the amendments.[9]

Success followed success. On June 7, Rhode Island, which ended its opposition to the union that year, surely surprised everyone by voting to ratify all but the salary amendment. Just as Madison had hoped, the addition of the Bill of Rights to the Constitution had ensured that "Rogues Island," like North Carolina, would become a respectable member of the United States. Vermont, which achieved statehood on March 4, 1791, ratified all twelve amendments that November. All eyes now turned to Madison's home state, Virginia.

Virginia's debates were protracted and, at key moments, influenced by Patrick Henry's erratic and unexplained behavior. Although the discussions began in 1789, no decision was reached until December 1791. When the first session of Congress adjourned in 1789, Senator Richard Henry Lee and Congressman William Grayson sent the state government copies of the twelve proposed amendments. In their cover letters, both men made clear they shared Patrick Henry's commitment to the supremacy of the states and his proud provincialism. The Bill of Rights, they declared, fell "far short of the wishes of our *Country.*" There could be little doubt, they added, that America was moving toward a consolidated empire in which the individual states would be abolished or made powerless. Still these two Virginians could not give up all hope for the ultimate success of their cause. They closed their report with this prediction: "unless a dangerous Apathy should invade the public mind, it will not be many years before a constitutional number of Legislatures will be found to *demand* a Convention" to prevent the annihilation of the state governments. This letter, with its dark predictions and persistent hopes, was published and widely circulated in other states.[10]

Patrick Henry and his avid followers were not willing to ratify the amendments, but there were signs that Henry's personal influence in the state government was ebbing. When he proposed that the house of delegates formally thank Grayson and Lee for their efforts, the legislature refused. Perhaps it was this rebuff that prompted Henry to abruptly leave Richmond and head home. But Antifederalists remained strong in the state senate, and here, even without Henry's charismatic presence, the opposition was able to prevent any further action on ratification in 1789.

As 1790 began, the prospect of ratification by Virginia looked bleak. The problem was Alexander Hamilton. On January 14 of that year, Secretary of the Treasury Hamilton submitted a *Report on Public Credit* that caused the defection of several key Federalists, including James Madison. The report called for the funding of the Revolutionary War debt, which he calculated at $54 million. This meant using federal revenues to make regular payments of the interest on the debt rather than paying off the principal as rapidly as possible. For Hamilton, establishing the nation's public credit was essential to the "individual and aggregate prosperity of the citizens of the United States." Few Virginians agreed. Hamilton made no effort to disguise the consequences of funding: the federal government would need to raise revenue steadily, something Hamilton proposed to accomplish, in part, through excise taxes. Not only foreign trade but also some forms of domestic production would thus be subject to federal taxation. The second piece of the funding proposal was far worse in the eyes of Virginians like Madison. For Hamilton intended to have the federal government assume the states' remaining war debts. It was not hard to see what this would mean: states would have little justification to impose taxes, but the federal government would have a pressing need to do so. The "power of the purse," as eighteenth-century men called it, would shift dramatically under Hamilton's scheme, and those who would benefit from the funding and assumption were certain to be northern businessmen. Henry Lee no doubt expressed the view of many Virginians when he said that Patrick Henry, who had often warned that oppression by the federal government was inevitable, was a prophet.[11]

For James Madison, assumption and funding posed a moral dilemma. Hamilton intended to honor the current holders of the debt certificates rather than their original holders. This meant that speculators would reap the benefits while ordinary farmers or military veterans who had sold their certificates when these were practically worthless would not. Madison was realistic enough to see that finding the original holders would be impractical if not impossible, yet he was repelled by the prospect of enriching speculators. Hamilton's programs and policies produced an economic trajectory for the nation that Madison could not support; the two friends who had once championed a new, energetic government had permanently parted ways.

In the end, Hamilton was victorious. Congress began its debate on his report on February 8; by the end of July a funding bill was a reality. That December, in a second report, Hamilton proposed a national bank. To his opponents, the secretary of the treasury was rapidly importing the very English financial structures and fiscal policies that had led to tyranny and abuse.[12]

Federalists had lost much ground in Virginia, yet Antifederalists had no reason to feel triumphant. By 1791, their hope that the Constitution could be significantly altered had faded and they were on the defensive, struggling unsuccessfully to block Hamilton's policies. Assessing the political situation, the remaining Virginia Federalists decided to cautiously reopen the discussion of the Bill of Rights. Their strategy was to carefully divorce ratification from any support for the federal government's fiscal policies. Their cause was helped when, once again, on December 7, Patrick Henry abruptly abandoned Richmond without explanation. At long last, on December 15, 1791, Virginia ratified all twelve amendments. Henry could only regret that Virginia had been "outwitted" once again.[13]

On December 30, 1791, President George Washington informed Congress that the requisite eleventh state, his own Virginia, had ratified. Because the original amendments one and two did not receive the necessary votes, they had failed; numbers three to twelve now became Amendments 1 to 10.

On March 1, 1792, another Virginian, Secretary of State Thomas Jefferson, notified the governors that these ten amendments were officially approved. It was perhaps a measure of the declining interest in this protracted struggle that Jefferson put news of legislation on fishing and on the post office ahead of the announcement that a Bill of Rights had been added to the Constitution.

Despite the battles in Massachusetts and Virginia, despite the fiery attacks in the Pennsylvania press, despite the quixotic hopes still held by some Antifederalists that a new convention could become a reality, and despite many federalists' continued sense that the delineation of rights had been unnecessary, ratification had proceeded relatively quickly. The Constitution now had its Bill of Rights.

XIII

———

Whether Federalist or Antifederalist, nationalist or provincial, the men who led the new nation had much more in common than they might have conceded in the heat of their political and ideological struggles. Patrick Henry and Elbridge Gerry as much as George Washington and James Madison were committed to establishing a republic and to the principles of John Locke's theory of government as a social contract. Men who supported the Constitution and men who opposed it rejected monarchy with equal passion, and patriots of every stripe refused the legal establishment of an aristocracy. As members of the Revolutionary generation, they took pride in being citizens of a republic even if they were uncertain that their bold experiment would survive.

What, then, separated Federalist from Antifederalist? The most fundamental difference was this: supporters of a new constitution believed a strong national government would best serve the country; defenders of a continued league of friendship believed the people would be best served as citizens of their sovereign states. Localism thus clashed with nationalism—and the compromise devised by the Philadelphia convention satisfied no one fully.

The delegates to the Philadelphia convention called that compromise federalism. It was born out of a realistic assessment of what the voters would tolerate and what the sovereign states might be willing to accept: a federal system, granting certain explicit powers to the central government, leaving other powers and responsibilities to the existing state governments, and authorizing some powers to be shared by both. At the convention, Alexander Hamilton declared it unworkable—and eight decades later, the Civil War almost proved him correct.

The men who wrote the Constitution argued that America was in crisis: its trade and commerce with the outside world were in the doldrums; its internal commerce was virtually paralyzed by state rivalries; its credit at home and abroad was an embarrassment and a hindrance to economic growth; its borders were unsecured against attack by enemy nations; and its citizens and political structure were unprotected against the dangers of insurrection and anarchy from within. These men believed the Confederation was incapable of finding solutions to the problems that plagued the nation and condemned the state governments for their refusal to cooperate in trying. But their opponents saw a very different America. They conceded that there were problems, but their prognosis was decidedly positive. The country was making steady progress toward prosperity; its natural resources were bountiful; its population was young and hearty and growing through immigration and natural increase; and its citizens were largely content with their circumstances. Thus they saw no reason to sacrifice a league of friendship for what they feared would become a "consolidated" or national government. The Articles of Confederation, imperfect though they might be, embodied the goals of the Revolution and ought to be strengthened, not cast aside.

Even if the situation was temporarily dire, the defenders of the league of friendship created by the Articles believed the cost of the convention's solution was too high. They saw a host of dangers in the superimposition of this new government over local institutions. Men like Patrick Henry abhorred its power to tax and to regulate commerce, but the emotional heart of the opposition was the fear that a new central government would replicate all the oppressions of the British government whose control the revolutionaries had overthrown. Some opponents of the new government believed that this was the intent of the Philadelphia convention. Others believed that it would be the inevitable, if unintended, consequence of a consolidated government. To these men, there was no better proof of impending tyranny than the convention's refusal to include a bill of rights in its Constitution.

The men who came to be called Antifederalists lost their battle against ratification of the new Constitution. In the wake of their defeat, they took on the role of watchdogs against signs of potential tyranny and any infringement of the people's rights and liberties. Although they accepted the Federalist victory, their leaders still felt it was their patriotic duty to severely limit the new government's power and authority, either through the calling of a second constitutional convention or through alterations passed by Congress. Their goal was nothing less than the evisceration of the powers of the federal government, but it was their call for a bill of rights that had won them popular support.

James Madison understood the propaganda value of the opposition's criticism—and he recognized the actual goals this criticism camouflaged. He also understood the tactical mistake his own side had made in rejecting out of hand George Mason's call for a bill of rights in the last days of the Philadelphia convention. It was Madison who decided to disarm the Antifederalists—and separate the leadership from its base—by proposing that the Federalist-controlled First Congress pass just such a bill of rights. This was a political move, doggedly if not brilliantly executed. To Madison's credit, he persevered in the face of opposition and even derision from the members of his own party who believed, after the Federalists won control of Congress, that the enemy had already been vanquished. He was not spared criticism, in private or in the press, for interrupting the important business of the House with his proposals for amendments.

Madison's strategy was relatively transparent to friends and foes alike. Not only would he steal the opposition's thunder, but he would control what was offered to the voters as amendments, carefully avoiding any challenge to the government's power to tax, regulate trade, or establish a court system. Yet if they understood his strategy, Madison's contemporaries in both camps wondered at his motivation. Was there more behind his insistence on interrupting the serious business of the House than his misguided belief that the Antifederalists continued to pose a threat? Some attributed his campaign for a bill of rights to his fear of being repudiated by the voters back home in Virginia. Others, more generously, attributed it to his desire to honor a campaign pledge made to those voters in 1788. Only a small number of friends may have realized that Madison was also struggling with one of the central problems of a republic: how to protect the liberties of minorities against the tyranny of the majority. Madison was less frightened in 1789 of an abuse of power by Congress or the executive branch than he was of the infringement of a minority's rights of conscience by its neighbors.

Madison's understanding of this problem, and his hope for a solution, grew slowly. He argued at first that a paper barrier against abuse from any source would be ineffectual. But he came to see that a clear statement of principle had the potential to become an internalized credo, a standard for behavior that checked an impulse to abuse the rights of others. In the end, he placed his hopes on the ability of a society to breed the angelic in merely mortal men.

The debates on Madison's amendments tell us much about the hopes and fears of spokesmen for both sides in this struggle. Articulate Antifederalists like Elbridge Gerry made clear the fears they harbored of a government that lost sight of who the true sovereigns in a republic were: the people. Federalists revealed their anxiety that any changes to the Constitution would lay bare the fragility of the enterprise, undermine the legitimacy of a new government, and add to the contempt in which European nations held the United States. The early effort by the Federalists in the House to delay each of these debates and their later desire to speed it to conclusion revealed their anxiety about the fate of the new government. For these men, designing a judicial system and establishing a revenue system were far more important than pledging not to abuse powers they insisted they did not have. They had promised the voters an energetic government—and they had told the world that they had designed one. Much depended, they believed, on their ability to prove it was so. The outbursts of anger by the House Antifederalists and their resort to obstructionism and delay revealed the frustrations of a political minority facing inevitable defeat.

In the course of these debates, men who—if they are known at all— are largely known by the offices they held or by the wealth they amassed, emerge as distinctive personalities. From the dignified but unassuming "Father" Sherman to the egotistical and clever Fisher Ames, from the defensive and suspicious Aedanus Burke to the sly, aggressive, brilliant Elbridge Gerry, we see the men who began our national history not as bronze statues in our parks and surely not as visionaries confidently shaping the world for generations yet to come, but as imperfect actors in an unpredictable drama.

It is difficult for Americans today to understand how tenuous the republic's survival seemed in 1789 and how heavily its fate weighed on the men of the First Congress and their leader in the executive office. No one could be certain whether the government over which George Washington was to preside would live up to Madison's hopes or down to Samuel Adams's fears. No one could be certain that it would not be crippled by internal enemies or conquered by external ones. What the members of the government did know was that they had few successful models to guide them—and many examples of failed republics to shake their confidence in the survival of their own. Indeed, history had taught them that republics were fragile, that even the noblest of leaders eventually succumbed to the lure of power, and that tyranny could easily poison political institutions.

History had also taught them that the people could degenerate into the mob, that loyalties to governments could be dissolved, and that violence always lay just below the surface even when civilized men argued over the laws they would live by. It is in this context that we must understand Madison's crusade to disarm the government's critics and enemies and to assure the people of the federal government's commitment to their liberties.

The Bill of Rights, like the Constitution itself, was conceived as a solution to an immediate peril. None of the men who played a role in creating it, not even James Madison, could envision the importance these ten amendments would have to future generations of Americans.

Epilogue

———

The Declaration of Independence and the first ten amendments to the Constitution are the two greatest written legacies of the Revolutionary generation. But it is sometimes forgotten that the men who gave us these documents composed them in response to particular crises of their own era. Jefferson's Declaration was written to justify a revolution; Madison's Bill of Rights was drafted to secure the loyalty of citizens wary of their new federal government. Yet these documents have outlived their original purposes and meanings in large part because they have been reinterpreted by later generations.

For the Revolutionary generation, the Declaration's opening was a simple restatement of Locke's theory of the social contract. It was followed by multiple examples of abuses by the king of England that broke the contract between ruler and citizens—and justified rebellion. But in the 1830s, the abolitionist movement reinterpreted the promise of life, liberty, and the pursuit of happiness as a justification for the emancipation of enslaved African Americans. Jefferson's stirring words were thus used to legitimate a crusade against slavery. When President Abraham Lincoln said that the Declaration embodied the noblest of our collective aspirations, its promise became the national credo. Although this concept of equality has sometimes been honored in the breach, it still stands today as an expression of our highest ideals.[1]

It took far longer for the Bill of Rights to become what it is today: the ultimate protector of our civil liberties. For almost seven decades after they were ratified, these first ten amendments to the Constitution were used, not to prevent abuse by any level of government, but to buttress arguments for state sovereignty. These arguments continued long after opposition to the Constitution itself had faded, for the boundaries between federal and state power remained unsettled. Many Americans were anxious about encroachment on the states' authority through what they considered unconstitutional extensions of federal power. It was this anxiety that had defeated Madison's effort to extend the first amendment's protections to cover abuses by the states. And, although the federalists had managed to block the addition of "expressly" in the tenth amendment, many political leaders stood ready to oppose the use of the "necessary and proper" clause or a broad interpretation of the Constitution by the federal government.

This readiness to challenge the authority of the federal government was evident in 1798, and the Bill of Rights was used to support this challenge. In that year, the Federalist majority in Congress passed a series of acts designed to tighten naturalization regulation, to rid the country of alien agitators, and to silence the intense opposition to the Adams administration that filled the press. These Alien and Sedition Acts, whose thinly veiled political goal was to weaken, if not destroy, the growing popularity of Jefferson's Republican party, were met with popular outrage. The federal government was accused of ignoring the first amendment's protection of free speech. It was also accused of asserting powers not explicitly granted by the Constitution. To the Republicans, as to the Antifederalists, "expressly" remained the unwritten modifier of the tenth amendment.

Virginia and Kentucky publicly challenged the constitutionality of all four of these 1798 acts. Their main focus was the Sedition Act, which gave the federal government the power to try, imprison, and impose fines on newspaper editors and contributors who attacked Adams's government.

Neither Virginia nor Kentucky sought a remedy from *federal* courts; instead, both states asserted their legislatures' right to deny the legality of these laws. In its resolutions, Virginia declared that Congress was exercising "a power not delegated by the Constitution, but on the contrary, expressly and positively forbidden by one of the amendments thereto." Kentucky went further. In words that Elbridge Gerry and Patrick Henry would have applauded, it reasserted opposition to a "consolidated" government. Its resolutions declared: "[T]he several states who formed that instrument [the Constitution], being sovereign and independent, have the unquestionable right to judge of its infraction; and that a nullification, by those [states], of all unauthorized acts . . . is the rightful remedy." Thomas Jefferson had drafted the Kentucky Resolutions, but it was James Madison, once a leading nationalist and author of the Bill of Rights, who wrote the Virginia Resolutions. No other states were willing to make this implicit threat of disunion, and thus the Alien and Sedition Acts went into effect.[2]

Under the Sedition Act at least a dozen newspaper editors and writers were indicted. By the time the act expired in 1801, many of the leading antiadministration newspapers had been eliminated. The Adams administration never acted on the powers granted it to deport aliens from nations at war with this country, although the Alien Enemies Act remained in effect well into the twentieth century. The Alien Friends Act, which allowed for the deportation of aliens from countries not at war with the United States, expired in 1800. The hated Sedition Act expired in 1801. The political consequences for the Federalists were disastrous and Jefferson's party swept into office in 1800. But the impact of the Virginia and Kentucky Resolutions reached far into the nineteenth century. In the decades before the Civil War, the threat of nullification remained part of the arsenal of the states against federal authority, and it reached its climax with the secessionist movement and the Civil War.

The Union victory in the Civil War led to a new, greatly expanded role for the guarantees of the Bill of Rights. Prompted by the desire to protect the rights and liberties of the recently emancipated African Americans, the fourteenth amendment was ratified in 1868. This amendment did what Madison could not do; it extended the umbrella of protection established in the Bill of Rights against actions by the states. The amendment declared, "No state shall make or enforce any law which shall abridge the privileges or immunities of citizens of the United States; nor shall any state deprive any person of life, liberty, or property, without due process of law; nor deny to any person within its jurisdiction the equal protection of the laws." The reach of the federal government was now greater than James Madison had ever hoped for, greater than most of his contemporaries could imagine, and certainly greater than many of his opponents would have tolerated.

The application of the due process clause of the fourteenth amendment released the potential of the Bill of Rights, and the results have been far-reaching. It led to victories in the civil rights struggle of the 1950s and 1960s and it frames many of the controversial struggles in our own day. Yet the ideological tug-of-war between state and federal government that Elbridge Gerry and James Madison represented has never completely ended. It found physical expression in the violence and bloodshed of the Civil War. Its revival could be seen in Little Rock, Arkansas, as the civil rights struggles of the 1950s began, and its capacity to endure can be seen in the many culture wars waged by modern Americans today. Many of the most divisive modern cultural issues raise those questions about the relationship of majority values and minority rights that so troubled James Madison. And the conflicts that ensue often take place in an arena where states' rights again do battle against the authority of the national government. James Madison might be puzzled by the content of these struggles but he would surely recognize the continuing tension between local and national sovereignty.

After nearly three centuries of debate, the one certainty is that these arguments over sovereignty are likely to continue. In giving us a federal republic, the founding generation left a legacy of unending struggle between the central government and the state governments. Yet it is important to remember that loyalties in this battle between states' rights and federal authority have never been constant; American's views and their motives have shifted as the context shifts, as new policies are proposed, and when political fortunes hang in the balance. Madison, the defender of an "energetic" national government and the author of the Bill of Rights in 1789, could emerge in 1798 as the champion of states' rights and the author of the Virginia Resolutions. His shift in loyalties reminds us that the meaning of federalism is always changing, never fixed.

Despite the fluidity of meaning that marks the history of federalism, the Bill of Rights has fulfilled James Madison's fervent hope that this "parchment barrier" would benefit the civic and moral development of the nation. It has proved a strong bulwark for our liberties and a safeguard against the majority's abuse of minorities. And it has established the vocabulary for our most critical discussions of, and fiercest debates over, who we are and what we think it is best to do.

Appendix

———

· *The Bill of Rights* ·

AMENDMENT I

Congress shall make no law respecting an establishment of religion, or prohibiting the free exercise thereof; or abridging the freedom of speech, or of the press; or the right of the people peaceably to assemble, and to petition the government for a redress of grievances.

AMENDMENT II

A well regulated militia, being necessary to the security of a free state, the right of the people to keep and bear arms, shall not be infringed.

AMENDMENT III

No soldier shall, in time of peace be quartered in any house, without the consent of the owner, nor in time of war, but in a manner to be prescribed by law.

AMENDMENT IV

The right of the people to be secure in their persons, houses, papers, and effects, against unreasonable searches and seizures, shall not be violated, and no warrants shall issue, but upon probable cause, supported by oath or affirmation, and particularly describing the place to be searched, and the persons or things to be seized.

AMENDMENT V

No person shall be held to answer for a capital, or otherwise infamous crime, unless on a presentment or indictment of a grand jury, except in cases arising in the land or naval forces, or in the militia, when in actual service in time of war or public danger; nor shall any person be subject for the same offense to be twice put in jeopardy of life or limb; nor shall be compelled in any criminal case to be a witness against himself, nor be deprived of life, liberty, or property, without due process of law; nor shall private property be taken for public use, without just compensation.

AMENDMENT VI

In all criminal prosecutions, the accused shall enjoy the right to a speedy and public trial, by an impartial jury of the state and district wherein the crime shall have been committed, which district shall have been previously ascertained by law, and to be informed of the nature and cause of the accusation; to be confronted with the witnesses against him; to have compulsory process for obtaining witnesses in his favor, and to have the assistance of counsel for his defense.

AMENDMENT VII

In suits at common law, where the value in controversy shall exceed twenty dollars, the right of trial by jury shall be preserved, and no fact tried by a jury, shall be otherwise reexamined in any court of the United States, than according to the rules of the common law.

AMENDMENT VIII

Excessive bail shall not be required, nor excessive fines imposed, nor cruel and unusual punishments inflicted.

AMENDMENT IX

The enumeration in the Constitution, of certain rights, shall not be construed to deny or disparage others retained by the people.

AMENDMENT X

The powers not delegated to the United States by the Constitution, nor prohibited by it to the states, are reserved to the states respectively, or to the people.

First. That there be prefixed to the Constitution a declaration, that all power is originally vested in, and consequently derived from, the people.

That Government is instituted and ought to be exercised for the benefit of the people; which consists in the enjoyment of life and liberty, with the right of acquiring and using property, and generally of pursuing and obtaining happiness and safety.

That the people have an indubitable, unalienable, and indefeasible right to reform or change their Government, whenever it be found adverse or inadequate to the purposes of its institution.

Secondly. That in article 1st, section 2, clause 3, these words be struck out, to wit: "The number of Representatives shall not exceed one for every thirty thousand, but each State shall have at least one Representative, and until such enumeration shall be made"; and that in place thereof be inserted these words, to wit: "After the first actual enumeration, there shall be one Representative for every thirty thousand, until the number amounts to————, after which the proportion shall be so regulated by Congress, that the number shall never be less than————, nor more than————, but each State shall, after the first enumeration, have at least two Representatives; and prior thereto."

Thirdly. That in article 1st, section 6, clause 1, there be added to the end of the first sentence, these words, to wit: "But no law varying the compensation last ascertained shall operate before the next ensuing election of Representatives."

Fourthly. That in article 1st, section 9, between clauses 3 and 4, be inserted these clauses, to wit: The civil rights of none shall be abridged on account of religious belief or worship, nor shall any national religion be established, nor shall the full and equal rights of conscience be in any manner, or on any pretext, infringed.

The people shall not be deprived or abridged of their right to speak, to write, or to publish their sentiments; and the freedom of the press, as one of the great bulwarks of liberty, shall be inviolable.

The people shall not be restrained from peaceably assembling and consulting for their common good; nor from applying to the Legislature by petitions, or remonstrances, for redress of their grievances.

The right of the people to keep and bear arms shall not be infringed; a well armed and well regulated militia being the best security of a free country: but no person religiously scrupulous of bearing arms shall be compelled to render military service in person.

No soldiers shall in time of peace be quartered in any house without the consent of the owner; nor at any time, but in a manner warranted by law.

No person shall be subject, except in cases of impeachment, to more than one punishment or one trial for the same offence; nor shall be compelled to be a witness against himself; nor be deprived of life, liberty, or property, without due process of law; nor be obliged to relinquish his property, where it may be necessary for public use, without a just compensation.

Excessive bail shall not be required, nor excessive fines imposed, nor cruel and unusual punishments inflicted.

The rights of the people to be secured in their persons, their houses, their papers, and their other property, from all unreasonable searches and seizures, shall not be violated by warrants issued without probable cause, supported by oath or affirmation, or not particularly describing the places to be searched, or the persons or things to be seized.

In all criminal prosecutions, the accused shall enjoy the right to a speedy and public trial, to be informed of the cause and nature of the accusation, to be confronted with his accusers, and the witnesses against him; to have a compulsory process for obtaining witnesses in his favor; and to have the assistance of counsel for his defence.

The exceptions here or elsewhere in the Constitution, made in favor of particular rights, shall not be so construed as to diminish the just importance of other rights retained by the people, or as to enlarge the powers delegated by the Constitution; but either as actual limitations of such powers, or as inserted merely for greater caution.

Fifthly. That in article 1st, section 10, between clauses 1 and 2, be inserted this clause, to wit:

No State shall violate the equal rights of conscience, or the freedom of the press, or the trial by jury in criminal cases.

Sixthly. That, in article 3d, section 2, be annexed to the end of clause 2d, these words, to wit:

But no appeal to such court shall be allowed where the value in controversy shall not amount to————dollars: nor shall any fact triable by jury, according to the course of common law, be otherwise re-examinable than may consist with the principles of common law.

Seventhly. That in article 3d, section 2, the third clause be struck out, and in its place be inserted the clauses following, to wit:

The trial of all crimes (except in cases of impeachments, and cases arising in the land or naval forces, or the militia when on actual service, in time of war or public danger) shall be by an impartial jury of freeholders of the vicinage, with the requisite of unanimity for conviction, of the right of challenge, and other accustomed requisites; and in all crimes punishable with loss of life or member, presentment or indictment by a grand jury shall be an essential preliminary, provided that in cases of crimes committed within any county which may be in possession of an enemy, or in which a general insurrection may prevail, the trial may by law be authorized in some other county of the same State, as near as may be to the seat of the offence.

In cases of crimes committed not within any county, the trial may by law be in such county as the laws shall have prescribed. In suits at common law, between man and man, the trial by jury, as one of the best securities to the rights of the people, ought to remain inviolate.

Eighthly. That immediately after article 6th, be inserted, as article 7th, the clauses following, to wit:

The powers delegated by this Constitution are appropriated to the departments to which they are respectively distributed: so that the Legislative Department shall never exercise the powers vested in the Executive or Judicial, nor the Executive exercise the powers vested in the Legislative or Judicial, nor the Judicial exercise the powers vested in the Legislative or Executive Departments.

The powers not delegated by this Constitution, nor prohibited by it to the States, are reserved to the States respectively.

Ninthly. That article 7th be numbered as article 8th.

Biographies

————

Members of the First Federal Congress[1]

MEMBERS OF THE SENATE

———

BASSETT, RICHARD (1745–1815)
Senator from Delaware; Antifederalist

Bassett's father was a tavern keeper who deserted the family. Bassett was raised by a relative, Peter Lawson, who left him his estate, Bohemia Manor. Bassett read law in Philadelphia and set up his practice in 1770 in Dover, Delaware. He was both a successful lawyer and a successful planter. During the Revolutionary War, he captained a Dover cavalry militia troop and served on the Delaware council of safety. He both raised and staffed the Delaware Continentals, one of the largest battalions in the Continental Army. He was a delegate to the Philadelphia convention, where he said virtually nothing and sat on no committees. He was a delegate to the state ratifying convention, voting in favor of adoption of the Constitution. At the age of forty-four, Bassett was elected to the First Federal Congress as a senator, a position he held until 1793. From 1793 until 1799 he was the chief justice of the court of common pleas, and from 1799 until 1801, he served as governor of Delaware. Bassett was one of the "midnight judges" appointed by President Adams in 1801 but denied the bench by President Jefferson. A convert to Methodism, Bassett devoted much of his energy and wealth to his faith. Though stout, he was very fashionable; during his months at the

Philadelphia convention, the always observant William Pierce described him as "a Man of plain sense," with "modesty enough to hold his tongue."

BUTLER, PIERCE (1744–1822)
Senator from South Carolina; Federalist

Born into an aristocratic Irish family, Butler came to America in 1758 as an officer in the British army. He resigned his commission and settled in Charleston as a planter, owning ten thousand acres by the eve of the Revolution. Much of his estate and his fortune was lost in the British occupation of South Carolina. During the war he was an officer in the state militia and was instrumental in reorganizing the state's defenses. When Charleston fell to the British, Butler was part of the resistance movement, working with Francis Marion and Thomas Sumter. When the war ended, he was one of the strongest voices for reconciliation with his fellow Americans who had supported the Loyalist cause. Butler was both a member of the Confederation Congress and a delegate to the Philadelphia convention, where he was an advocate for yeoman farmers but also one of the strongest supporters of concessions to benefit slave owners. His observations on his fellow delegates were sometimes blunt, sometimes harsh, but always astute. At the age of forty-five, he was elected to the First Federal Congress, serving as a senator from 1789 to 1796; he served again from 1802 to 1804. Following the death of Alexander Hamilton in a duel with Aaron Burr, Burr was a guest at Butler's plantation. By the end of his life, Butler was one of the wealthiest men in the United States, owning plantations in several states including Georgia. Men who knew him often described him as eccentric, an aristocratic planter who championed the common man. Butler was married to the actress Fanny Kemble, whose abolitionist views contrasted sharply with his defense of slavery. After a turbulent eleven years, Kemble deserted him.

CARROLL, CHARLES (1737–1832)

Senator from Maryland; Federalist

Born into a distinguished Catholic family, but to parents who were not yet married, Carroll received an education at a Jesuit college in Maryland and the College of St. Omer in France. He studied civil law at the College of Louis le Grand in Reims and common law in London. He returned to Maryland in 1765. As the owner of a large plantation, Carroll was a slaveholder, despite his belief that slavery was wrong. He did free his own slaves at his death; and in the 1820s, the ninety-one year-old Carroll served as president of the Auxiliary State Colonization Society of Maryland, an organization devoted to relocating black Americans to freedom in Liberia. Maryland law excluded Catholics from public office, but after the Revolution this ban was removed. Carroll was a delegate to the Revolutionary convention in Maryland in 1775, and during the war he served on the Board of War and as a delegate to the Continental Congress, where he was a signer of the Declaration of Independence. In Maryland he served in the state senate from 1777 to 1800. He was elected to the First Federal Congress at the age of fifty-two and served until 1792. When he retired to private life, he was instrumental in the founding of the Baltimore & Ohio railroad company. He was the last surviving signatory to the Declaration. Carroll was immortalized in his state's song, "Maryland, My Maryland": "Thou wilt not cower in the dust / Maryland! My Maryland! / Thy beaming sword shall never rust / Maryland! My Maryland! / Remember Carroll's sacred trust / Remember Howard's warlike thrust."

DALTON, TRISTRAM (1738–1817)

Senator from Massachusetts; Federalist

Born in Massachusetts and a graduate of Harvard College, where he was a classmate of John Adams, Dalton was admitted to the bar but chose not to open a practice. Instead, he became a very successful merchant, running a privateer supply fleet for the revolutionaries during the war. Dalton was elected to his state's house of representatives from 1782 to 1785 and was chosen as speaker in 1784. Although he was chosen for the Confederation Congress in 1783 and again in 1784, he did not attend. In 1785, he became a state senator, and was a delegate to the state ratifying convention. He was a strong supporter of the Constitution, which he judged "a masterpiece."[2] In 1789, at the age of fifty-one, he became a member of the First Federal Congress, traveling to New York "in his private carriage, with driver and footman in livery, and his body servant, African Caesar, his slave, in constant attendance." Because his wife loved city life, Dalton sold his property in Essex County, bought a home in Georgetown, and invested heavily in land in the new national capital, Washington, D.C. An unscrupulous agent handled his investment, however, and he was reduced to poverty.[3] His biographer described Dalton as "well-built, large and robust, with a fine erect figure, an open, benevolent and handsome face, and that natural air of superiority which implies a fine organization." His "mental powers," however, "were not remarkable."[4]

ELLSWORTH, OLIVER (1745–1807)
Senator from Connecticut; Federalist

Ellsworth began his college education at Yale but transferred to the College of New Jersey (Princeton), where he studied theology. After graduation he turned to law and was admitted to the bar in 1771. In 1778, he was sent to represent his state in the Continental Congress; later, he served in the Confederation Congress. He became a judge of the Connecticut superior court in 1785 and served until 1789. He was a delegate to the Philadelphia convention, where he was instrumental in shaping the Connecticut Compromise, and at the age of forty-four, entered the First Federal Congress as a senator. In 1796 he resigned this office to become the chief justice of the United States until his retirement in 1800. He was an envoy extraordinary and minister plenipotentiary to France from 1799 until his return to the United States in 1801. From 1801 until the year of his death, he was once again a member of the Connecticut governor's council. William Pierce, who commented on many of his fellow delegates to the Philadelphia convention, described Ellsworth as "a gentleman of a clear, deep, and copious understanding, eloquent in . . . public debate . . . very happy in reply, and choice in selecting such parts of his adversary's arguments as he finds makes the strongest impressions, in order to take off the force of them so as to admit the power of his own."[5]

ELMER, JONATHAN (1745–1817)
Senator from New Jersey; Federalist

A graduate of the first medical class of the College of Philadelphia (University of Pennsylvania) in 1769, Elmer established a practice in Bridgeton, New Jersey. He was made high sheriff of Cumberland County in 1772. A supporter of the Revolution, Elmer was made a captain of a light infantry company in 1775, but physical frailty prevented him from seeing active duty. He was a member of the Continental Congress and the Confederation Congress beginning in 1777 and a member of his state council in 1780 and 1784. He became a trustee of the College of New Jersey (Princeton) and served in that capacity from 1782 to 1795. He became the president of the state medical society in 1787. He entered the First Federal Congress at the age of forty-four and held his seat until 1791. He returned to state service as judge of the county court of common pleas from 1802 to 1804 and again in 1813 but was forced to resign the following year because of ill health.

FEW, WILLIAM (1748–1793)
Senator from Georgia; Antifederalist

Few was born in Baltimore but his father moved the family to North Carolina when William was ten years old. The Fews' modest circumstances made formal education impossible. In 1771, Few, his father, and his brother James became members of the "Regulators," frontiersmen who protested the unequal treatment of backcountry farmers by the coastal elite. His brother was hanged because of his participation in the protests and the family then fled to Georgia. William remained behind to see to his father's affairs, but by 1776, he too was in Georgia. Here, he was admitted to the bar and began a practice in Augusta. During the Revolutionary War, he became a lieutenant colonel in the dragoons. In 1776, he entered politics, serving in the Georgia provincial congress and then in the assembly and acting as surveyor general and Indian commissioner as well. He was in the Continental Congress by 1780 and then served seven years in the Confederation Congress. He was a delegate to the Philadelphia convention, although he missed many of its sessions because of his congressional duties. He was a member of the state ratifying convention and supported the Constitution's adoption. At the age of forty-one, he became a senator in the First Federal Congress; when his term ended, he returned to state office. But at the age of fifty-two, he resigned his positions in Georgia and moved to New York City, the home of his wife, and here he was elected to the state assembly in 1802. He also became a director of the Manhattan Bank and the president of City Bank. James Marshall, brother of jurist John Marshall, said of Few: "He was one of those men, 'few and far between' who effect more by solid weight of character than many can by eloquent speech or restless action."[6] And William Pierce noted, "Mr. Few possesses a strong natural Genius."

GRAYSON, WILLIAM (c. 1740–1790)
Senator from Virginia; Antifederalist

Orphaned by 1757, Grayson became the ward of his older brother, Benjamin. He attended the College of Philadelphia (University of Pennsylvania) but did not graduate. He studied the classics at the University of Oxford and law in London. Returning to Virginia he set up a legal practice in Dumfries. Described as a "very large and remarkably handsome man, of noble appearance and manners," Grayson married Eleanor Smallwood, the sister of the governor of Maryland. During the Revolution, he was commissioned as a Lieutenant Colonel and served as an aide-de-camp to General Washington. He sat in the Virginia house of delegates from 1784 to 1785 and then became a member of the Confederation Congress. In late 1786, Grayson was seriously ill with gout. James Monroe described his condition to James Madison, saying that Grayson had "an extraordinary disease . . . he is often delirious, is afflicted with strange fancies and apprehensions. . . . It is supposed by some to be floating gout." But Grayson had recovered sufficiently by the end of the year to return to Congress. He was a delegate to the state ratifying convention, where he opposed adoption of the Constitution, saying, "I prefer a complete consolidation to a partial one, but a federal government to either." At the age of forty-nine, Grayson was elected to the First Federal Congress, but a return of gout prevented him from attending until late May. He served as a senator until his death in 1790.[7]

GUNN, JAMES (1753–1801)
Senator from Georgia; Federalist

Born in Virginia, Gunn settled in Georgia, where he was admitted to the bar and established a practice in Savannah. He served as a captain of the dragoons during the Revolutionary War and in the county and state militias, rising to the rank of brigadier general in the militia. He was elected to the Confederation Congress in 1787 but did not serve. He entered the First Federal Congress at the age of thirty-six, and held his seat until 1801. He was implicated in the Yazoo Land Fraud and as a result, angry Savannah citizens burned him in effigy in 1795. Gunn had a reputation as a quick-tempered man with an exaggerated sense of honor. He had several confrontations that ended in violence, in one case using a whip to attack a military man of lower rank who had offended him by singing a song with a British tune. Gunn called the man "a stinking puppy," a serious insult in the eighteenth century.[8] When he discovered in 1791 that his wife was having an affair, his friend Pierce Butler of South Carolina advised against challenging her lover to a duel. Butler assured Gunn, "Your character as a Man of spirit is as fixed as fate" and thus no shame would come to him if he did not avenge his honor.[9]

HENRY, JOHN (1750–1798)
Senator from Maryland; Federalist

Henry graduated from the College of New Jersey in 1769 and went on to study law at the Inns of Court in London. Returning to America in 1775, he established a law practice in Dorchester County, Maryland. He served in the Maryland house of delegates from 1777 to 1780 and was a delegate to the Continental Congress and Confederation Congress from 1778 to 1786; in the latter, he was a member of the committee that prepared the ordinance for the government of the Northwest Territory. He was sent to the First Federal Congress at the age of thirty-nine and served through 1797. In that year, he was elected governor of Maryland, but he resigned in 1798 because of bad health. In response to his resignation, the Maryland house of delegates praised him for his "upright and virtuous heart" and assured him of the "grateful sense of your countrymen for more than twenty years' honorable and meritorious service." [10]

IZARD, RALPH (1741/42–1804)
Senator from South Carolina; Federalist

Orphaned when a small child, Izard spent most of his childhood and youth studying in England. He returned to America in 1764, but soon went abroad once again, moving first to London and later to Paris. The Continental Congress appointed him commissioner to the court of Tuscany in 1776 but he was recalled in 1779. In 1777, his anxiety over the fate of his country contributed to a debilitating episode of gout that left him bedridden for several months. He settled on his large estate in South Carolina in 1780 but spent many of his summers in New York. He pledged that estate to pay for warships during the Revolutionary War. In 1782, he became a member of the Confederation Congress. At the age of forty-eight he was sent to the First Federal Congress, where he served from 1789 until 1795. While a senator, Izard defended slavery, opposed the Bill of Rights, and helped to organize the federal court system. Izard then retired from public life. He soon suffered "a dreadful malady" that left him paralyzed on one side. Izard rewarded one of his slaves who attended him in his illness by giving him his freedom. He was a founder of the College of Charleston. Izard was described by Langdon Cheves as a man "of high ability and spirit, of fine appearance, finished manners and Taste in art and literature." [11]

JOHNSON, WILLIAM SAMUEL (1727–1819)

Senator from Connecticut; Federalist

Tutored by his father, a well-known Anglican clergyman, Johnson went on to graduate from Yale and Harvard. He pursued a career in law despite his father's hope that he would become a minister, and practiced in Stratford, Connecticut. He became a member of his colony's house of representatives in 1761 and went on to serve in the colony's upper house. He was a delegate to the Stamp Act Congress in 1765, but was not a committed revolutionary; he had many friends in England and a strong commitment to the Anglican Church and thus found it difficult to choose a side. He would not serve in the continental congress despite being elected in 1774 and preferred to play a role as a peacemaker between the British and the Americans. After the war, he reentered elective politics, serving in the Confederation Congress in 1785–1787. He played a major role at the Philadelphia convention, speaking often, although, according to William Pierce, there was "something in the tone of his voice not pleasing to the ear." Johnson worked for ratification of the Constitution in his home state. He became a senator—and one of the oldest members—in the First Federal Congress at the age of sixty-two. In 1791, he resigned his office because he wished to devote his time more fully to the presidency of Columbia College. He retired from this position in 1800, and at the age of seventy-three married for the second time. To Johnson is attributed the quote: "Patriotism is the last refuge of a scoundrel."

KING, RUFUS (1755–1827)

Senator from New York; Federalist

Born in Scarborough, Maine, then a part of Massachusetts, King was the son of a prosperous merchant whose home was ransacked by a mob during the Stamp Act crisis. Although their father would become a Loyalist, King and his brothers supported the Revolution. King graduated from Harvard College and began to read law, but his studies were interrupted in 1778 when he volunteered for militia duty in the war. He served as an aide to General John Sullivan. A civilian once more, King was admitted to the bar and began a legal practice in Newburyport, Massachusetts. He was elected to the state assembly in 1783 and served until 1785. He was sent to the Confederation Congress from 1784 to 1787 and was one of the youngest members there. In 1787 he was a delegate to the Philadelphia convention, where he impressed fellow delegate William Pierce as "A Man much distinguished for his eloquence and great parliamentary talents." Pierce commented on King's "peculiarly strong and rich . . . expression, clear and convincing . . . arguments." King also worked to see his home state ratify the Constitution. When he failed to be selected for the Senate from Massachusetts, he was urged by Alexander Hamilton to relocate to New York. Here, he was elected to the New York state assembly and in 1789, at the age of only thirty-four, was chosen for the First Federal Congress. He served in this legislative body until 1796, when he was appointed U.S. minister to Great Britain. He held this post until 1803 and again from 1825 to 1826. He was the vice presidential candidate on the losing Federalist ticket in 1804 and again in 1808. In 1816, he lost the election for governor of New York to a member of the Jeffersonian Party. He was the last candidate for the presidency put forward by the Federalist Party before its demise. King was a longtime opponent of the expansion of slavery and of the slave trade. He possessed an enormous library of 3,500 volumes and two hundred bound volumes of pamphlets.

LANGDON, JOHN (1741–1819)
Senator from New Hampshire; Federalist

Born into a prosperous farm family, Langdon attended a local grammar school, worked as an apprentice clerk, and went to sea for a brief period. He became a successful merchant and a supporter of the Revolution. When morale was low in the state assembly during the war, Langdon rose to say: "I have two thousand dollars in specie, I will pledge my plate for as much more, I have eighty hogsheads of Tobago rum which will be sold for the service of the State. The country shall have it all, if we succeed in establishing our liberty I shall be repaid; if not property is of no value." He was a member of the Continental Congress in 1775 and 1776; and when the war began, he built privateers for operations against the British. He participated in the Battle of Bennington and commanded a company at Saratoga. In New Hampshire he served several terms as speaker of the state house of representatives before becoming a member of the state senate in 1784. He was a delegate to the Philadelphia convention, where he paid the expenses for himself and for his fellow delegate Nicholas Gilman, and a member of the state ratifying convention as well. William Pierce described him briefly as a "Man of considerable fortune, possess[ing] a liberal mind, and a good plain understanding." He was forty-eight when he became a senator in the First Federal Congress and served until 1801. He was offered the position of secretary of the navy by President Thomas Jefferson, but declined. He returned to the New Hampshire legislature in 1801 and became the state's governor from 1805 to 1811, with the exception of one year, 1809. Although he was asked to be the Jeffersonian Democratic candidate for vice president in 1812, age and ill health prompted him to refuse.

LEE, RICHARD HENRY (1732–1794)
Senator from Virginia; Antifederalist

Lee—whose younger brothers included Arthur Lee, an American diplomat, and Francis Lightfoot Lee, a leading revolutionary and a member of the Virginia senate and the Continental Congress—was born at the family plantation, Stratford Hall. He attended school in England, returning in 1751 to his home colony, Virginia. During the French and Indian War, Lee organized a group of neighborhood young men and attempted to have them join General Braddock's campaign, but the general refused to allow them to participate. By 1758 the twenty-six-year-old Lee was a member of the Virginia house of burgesses; he held his seat until 1775. When the Townshend Acts were passed in 1767, Lee publicly condemned them as "arbitrary, unjust, and destructive of that mutual beneficial connection which every good subject would wish to see preserved." Lee was a delegate to the Continental Congress from 1774 to 1779, and it was he who proposed the resolution for a Declaration of Independence. He was a signer of the Declaration and served during the war as a colonel in the Westmoreland militia. He was sent to the Confederation Congress in 1784 and served as its President that year; he returned in 1785 and 1787. He was a member of his state ratifying convention but opposed ratification of the Constitution, saying, "To say that a bad government must be established for fear of anarchy is really saying that we should kill ourselves for fear of dying." [12] He became a senator in the First Federal Congress at the age of fifty-seven and served until his resignation in 1792. He retired to private life on his plantation, Chantilly, where he remained until his death two years later.

MACLAY, WILLIAM (1737–1804)
Senator from Pennsylvania; Antifederalist

At the age of twenty-one, Maclay served as a lieutenant in an expedition to Fort Duquesne during the French and Indian War. Later he would serve in the Continental Army as a commissary during the American Revolution. Maclay studied law and was admitted to the bar but then became a surveyor employed by the Penn family. He was frequently elected to the state legislature in the 1780s, and became both a member of the executive council and a judge of the court of common pleas. Although at the age of fifty-two he was elected as a Federalist to the First Federal Congress, he almost immediately cast his lot with the Antifederalist faction in the Senate, declaring, "My mind revolts, in many instances, against the Constitution of the United States." He was an indefatigable journal keeper, and in his diary he drew many sharp and highly critical portraits of his colleagues, criticizing not only senators but the vice president and the president as well. He did not hesitate to find fault with whole states or regions of the country, writing, for example, "We Pennsylvanians act as if we believed that God made of one blood all families of the earth; but the Eastern people seem to think that he made none but New England folks." His dislike of New Yorkers led him to write: "These Yorkers are the vilest of people. Their vices have not the palliation of being manly. They resemble bad schoolboys who are unfortunate at play: they revenge themselves by telling enormous thumpers." At the age of fifty-two, he was selected to serve only a two-year term, and he failed in his effort to be chosen to serve again. He remained active in state politics, sitting in the Pennsylvania house of representatives from 1795 to 1797 and serving later on as a county judge.

MORRIS, ROBERT (1734–1806)
Senator from Pennsylvania; Federalist

Born near Liverpool, England, Morris emigrated at the age of thirteen and joined his father in Maryland. He was only briefly schooled, and as a young man he became an employee of a well-known shipping company. By 1754, he had become a partner in this firm. On the eve of the Revolution, his firm contracted to provide arms and ammunition to the American army. In 1775, he became a member of the Pennsylvania council of safety, the committee of correspondence, and the provincial assembly, and the Continental Congress. During the Revolution, he served the cause by devising means to raise funds and supplies for the army. In late 1776, he loaned the government $10,000 of his own money to assist in paying for the war. He also underwrote the operations of several privateer ships that ran the British blockades. He made a good deal of money from his efforts during the war, but his contributions earned him the right to be called the "financier of the American Revolution." Morris served in the state assembly from 1778 to 1781; in 1781 he became the national superintendent of finance under the Confederation and established the Bank of North America. He returned to the state assembly from 1785 to 1787 and was a delegate to the Philadelphia convention. Here, he impressed Willam Pierce greatly. "Although he is not learned," Pierce wrote, "yet he is as great as those who are." He was sent to the Senate by Pennsylvania's legislature at the age of fifty-five and served until 1795. He declined another senatorial term and he declined to serve as secretary of the treasury, supporting Alexander Hamilton for the post instead. Morris amassed one of the great fortunes of the era but his involvement in unsuccessful, often wild land speculation in the West led him to ruin. Writing to Alexander Hamilton in 1798, he admitted, "Starvation stares me in the face." He was imprisoned for debt that year and remained incarcerated until 1801. In 1781, the visiting marquis de Chastellux described Morris as "a large man, very simple in his manners; but his mind is subtle and acute, his head perfectly well organized, and he is as well versed in public affairs as in his own." [13]

PATERSON, WILLIAM (1745–1806)
Senator from New Jersey; Federalist

Born in Antrim, Ireland, Paterson immigrated to America at the age of two with his parents. The family settled in New Castle, Pennsylvania, but Paterson, who graduated from the College of New Jersey (Princeton), made his home in New Jersey. He studied law, passed the bar, and began a practice in New Bromley. He entered politics in 1775, as a delegate and secretary to the provincial congress, and later, in 1776 and 1777, served in the state council. He was a delegate to New Jersey's constitutional convention and became attorney general of the state from 1776 until 1783. He was elected to the Continental Congress but declined because of his duties as the state attorney general. He agreed, however, to serve as a delegate to the Philadelphia convention, where he was the leading proponent of the small states' proposal known as the New Jersey Plan. At the age of forty-four he became a senator in the First Federal Congress, but he resigned in 1790 to become governor of New Jersey. In 1793 he resigned from the governorship to become an associate justice of the US Supreme Court, a position he held until his death. William Pierce, who produced descriptions of most of the men at the Philadelphia convention, said that Paterson was short, modest, and unassuming in appearance but that he was one of those men "whose powers break in upon you, and create wonder and astonishment." [14]

READ, GEORGE (1733–1798)
Senator from Delaware; Federalist

Born into a prosperous Maryland family, Read attended the Philadelphia Academy, studied law and began his practice in New Castle, Delaware, at the age of nineteen. By the age of thirty, he was attorney general for lower Delaware, and in 1765 he became a member of the provincial assembly. He served in the Continental Congress from 1774 until 1777 and signed the Declaration of Independence. He was president of the state constitutional convention in 1776 and became vice president of Delaware under the new state constitution. In 1782, he became a judge of the U.S. court of appeals in admiralty cases. He was a delegate to the Philadelphia convention, where he was an outspoken champion of the rights of the smaller states. Fellow delegate William Pierce acknowledged Read's legal expertise but noted that "his powers of oratory are fatiguing and tiresome to the last degree; his voice is feeble and his articulation so bad that few can have patience to attend him." At the age of fifty-six, he entered the First Federal Congress, and he remained a senator until 1793, when he became chief justice of Delaware. He held this position until his death. Read was tall, slight, and handsome, and dressed elegantly; he was wearing amethyst-studded shoe buckles when he signed the Declaration of Independence.

SCHUYLER, PHILIP JOHN (1733–1804)
Senator from New York; Federalist

Schuyler, whose father died on the eve of his son's seventh birthday, grew up in Albany and on the family farm at the Flats. At the age of fifteen he was sent to New Rochelle to be educated by a French Protestant minister. By 1751, however, he had begun to show symptoms of both gout and pleurisy that would bother him throughout his life. At twenty-two, he married Catherine Van Rensselaer, the daughter of one of New York's manor lords; they had fifteen children, among them Elizabeth Schuyler, who married Alexander Hamilton. In 1755, he served as a captain in a militia company that built fortifications north of Albany to protect the city from French and Indian enemies. Later, as a major, he was sent to England to settle colonial claims. In his private life, he ran a successful lumber business and built the first flax mill in America. By 1761 he was wealthy enough to create his own landed estate, Schuyler Mansion. He entered politics as a member of the New York assembly in 1768 and went on to serve in the Continental Congress. During the Revolutionary War he was one of the four major generals in the Continental Army, serving from 1775 until he resigned in 1779. He returned to political life in 1780 as a member of the New York state senate, serving until 1784 and again from 1786 until 1790. He was fifty-six when he entered the Senate of the First Federal

Congress; he served from 1789 until 1791 and again from 1797 to early 1798, when an attack of gout forced him to resign.

STRONG, CALEB (1745–1819)
Senator from Massachusetts; Federalist

A graduate of Harvard College, Strong studied law and began his practice in 1772, eventually becoming one of the most successful attorneys in Hampshire County. During the Revolution, he served as a member of the state's committee of correspondence and safety; and from 1776 to 1778, he was a member of the state senate. He was elected to the Continental Congress in 1780 but did not attend. He was a delegate to the Philadelphia convention, where William Pierce noted that, while Strong had the esteem of his colleagues, he was a "feeble" speaker, "and without confidence." Strong supported adoption of the Constitution in his state ratifying convention and, at the age of forty-four, became a senator in the First Federal Congress. He served in that capacity from 1789 until 1796, when he resigned. He became governor of Massachusetts in 1800 and served until 1807; he was reelected to this position in 1812 and served until 1816. Strong opposed the War of 1812 and refused, while governor, to allow the state militia to be placed under army command.

WINGATE, PAINE (1739–1838)
Senator from New Hampshire; Antifederalist

Born in Massachusetts, Wingate graduated from Harvard College in 1759 and was ordained a minister in the Congregational Church four years later. He had pulpits in both Hampton Falls and Stratham, New Hampshire, but also farmed. He was a member of the state constitutional convention of 1781 and a member of New Hampshire's house of representatives in 1783. He served one year in the Confederation Congress before being elected to the Senate at the age of fifty. He remained a senator until 1793 and then became a member of the House of Representatives until 1795. He served as a judge on his state's superior court between 1798 and 1809 and then retired from political life to farm. Following James Madison's death in 1836, Wingate was one of only two remaining survivors of the Continental Congress.

MEMBERS OF THE
HOUSE OF REPRESENTATIVES

———

AMES, FISHER (1758–1808)
Representative from Massachusetts; Federalist

When Ames was only six his father died and the family was reduced to poverty. His mother recognized Ames's intellectual abilities and managed to give him a classical education. He was precocious, studying Latin by the time he was six and entering college at the age of twelve. He graduated from Harvard College, and for several years taught school in order to support his widowed mother. Later he studied law and set up a practice in Dedham, Massachusetts. His political career began in 1788 with election to the Massachusetts house of representatives and to the state ratifying convention. He served in the First through the Fourth Congresses and then retired from the federal government to resume his law practice in Dedham. Ames was widely acknowledged for his oratorical skill and his political writings, which appeared in the Boston newspapers. His eloquence in the Massachusetts legislature in 1788 prompted his election at the age of thirty to the First Congress in 1789, in a surprising victory over Samuel Adams. He served in Congress until 1796, when he retired to take up his legal practice once again and to serve as a member of the

Massachusetts governor's council. Ames was witty, often judgmental, and remarkably self-confident, but his eloquence in debate earned him the respect of his colleagues. He was a social conservative, wary of the excesses of democracy. In his view, "Popular reason does not always know how to act right, nor does it always act right when it knows."

BALDWIN, ABRAHAM (1754–1807)
Representative from Georgia; Antifederalist

Baldwin was born in Connecticut, the son of a blacksmith who had twelve children and borrowed money to send Baldwin to Yale. Here, he studied theology, preparing for the ministry. During the Revolutionary War, he served as a chaplain and studied law. In 1784 he moved to Augusta, Georgia, where he wrote the charter for the University of Georgia and served as its president from 1786 to 1801. He was a member of the Continental Congress and a delegate to the Philadelphia convention in 1787. He became a member of the House at the age of thirty-five and served from 1789 until 1799, when he was elected to the Senate. Baldwin never married but he did assume custody of six of his younger half siblings when his father died. In a eulogy delivered when Baldwin died at the age of fifty-three, he was praised for his "infinite labor and patience." His conservative nature was reflected in his favorite saying: "Take care, hold the wagon back; there is more danger of its running too fast than of its going too slow."

BENSON, EGBERT (1746–1833)
Representative from New York; Federalist

Benson was the son of a New York brewer and his Dutch wife. He was raised by his grandmother, who taught him to speak Dutch, and throughout his life he remained proud of this heritage. Benson graduated from King's College (now Columbia University) in 1765 and was admitted to the bar in New York City. He was a member of the local committee of safety during the Revolutionary War, and soon after independence was declared he was appointed the first attorney general of his state, an office he held until 1789. Benson served in the New York legislature, in the Continental Congress, and in New York's ratifying convention in 1788. He was elected to the First Federal Congress at the age of forty-three, winning a largely Dutch Antifederalist district by only ten votes. He served in the House until 1793. He became a judge of the supreme court of New York in 1794, a seat he held until 1801. He also served as the first president of the New-York Historical Society. Benson was known for his terse, unadorned style of speech, and he spoke rarely during his time in the Congress. A friend described him as a handsome man who knew "the pleasures of the table" and how to amuse his dinner mates with his anecdotes. He was awkward in the presence of women, however, and he remained a bachelor throughout his life.

BLAND, THEODORICK (1742–1790)
Representative from Virginia; Antifederalist

Bland was educated in England and studied medicine in Edinburgh. In 1759 he returned to Virginia, where he established his medical practice in Prince George County. During the Revolutionary War, he served in the Continental Army as a captain of the First Troop of Virginia Cavalry. He was a delegate to the Continental Congress from 1780 to 1783 and a member of the Virginia house of delegates from 1786 to 1788. At his state ratifying convention he voted against the ratification of the Constitution. He was elected to the first House of Representatives at the age of forty-seven, and served until his death the following year. In 1781, the marquis of Chastellux described Bland as tall and handsome, although in later years he grew fat. He had a delicate constitution and a dignified manner, and, though not a man of exceptional intellect, he did have creative aspirations that led him to write a poem commemorating the Battle of Lexington.

BOUDINOT, ELIAS (1740–1821)
Representative from New Jersey; Federalist

Boudinot, a descendant of Huguenots and the brother of one of America's first published female poets, Annis Boudinot, received a classical education and studied law with the man who would become his brother-in-law, Richard Stockton. After admission to the bar, he began a practice in Elizabethtown, New Jersey. By 1772 he was a member of the board of trustees of what would later become Princeton University. During the Revolutionary War, he served as commissary general of prisoners. In 1781, he became a delegate to the Confederation Congress and thus a signer of the Treaty of Paris, which ended the war. At the age of forty-nine, he was elected to the First Federal Congress, where he was recognized for his eloquence and intelligence. Boudinot served in the House until 1795, when he became director of the U.S. Mint. After his resignation from this directorship, he devoted himself to the study of biblical literature and to philanthropy. He had earned a fortune through investments and land speculation and donated generously to the city of Philadelphia, providing thirteen thousand acres for parks and other city needs. Boudinot was a strong supporter of missionary work and a devout Presbyterian. He was one of the founders of the American Bible Society and the author of *The Age of Revelation*, written as a rebuttal to Thomas Paine's *The Age of Reason*. Boudinot was tall and handsome in his youth, but his portrait of 1817 shows a balding, and heavyset man of seventy-seven. Boudinot supported the rights of African Americans and Indians and sponsored students at the Board School for Indians in Connecticut. One of these students, Gallegina Watie, asked for and received permission to adopt the name of his benefactor. As Elias Boudinot, this Cherokee Indian became the editor of the first newspaper of the Cherokee nation.

BROWN, JOHN (1757–1805)
Representative from Virginia; Antifederalist

Brown, the son of a Presbyterian minister from Ireland, attended Washington College (now Washington and Lee University) and the College of New Jersey (Princeton), but left school because of the Revolutionary War. He ultimately completed his education at the College of William and Mary and went on to study law with Thomas Jefferson. He was admitted to the bar in 1782 and set up a practice in Kentucky, which was then a part of Virginia. He served as a representative from the Kentucky district in the Virginia senate and in the 1787 and 1788 Confederation Congresses. He was elected at the age of thirty-two as an antiadministration member of the first federal House of Representatives and served until his election to the federal Senate in 1793 from the new state of Kentucky. He was said to be both eloquent and punctual during his political career.

BURKE, AEDANUS (1743–1802)
Representative from South Carolina; Antifederalist

Born in Galway, Ireland, Burke was educated at the theological College of St. Omer, France. He immigrated to the American colonies and settled in Charleston, South Carolina, where he practiced law. In 1778 he was appointed a judge of the state supreme court, and after a two-year hiatus while he served in his state militia during the Revolutionary War, he returned to the bench. He was a member of the South Carolina ratifying convention, where he opposed the Constitution, and soon afterward was elected to the House of Representatives at the age of forty-six as an antiadministration member. Burke was a vocal critic of any institution he believed to be aristocratic and wrote a widely distributed pamphlet attacking the Society of the Cincinnati, an organization created by former Revolutionary War officers. Burke charged that the men who joined the society were creating an incipient aristocratic class by restricting membership to themselves and their sons. Burke was famous for his wit but also for an eccentricity reflected in his tendency to see conspiracies afoot in the new republic. Burke declined to run for reelection to the House in 1790 because South Carolina's legislature had passed a law prohibiting its judges from leaving the state. In 1799, he was elected chancellor of the South Carolina courts of equity, a position he held until his death.

CADWALADER, LAMBERT (1742–1823)
Representative from New Jersey; Federalist

Cadwalader was born near Trenton, New Jersey, the descendant of a Welsh immigrant. He attended an academy run by Dr. Francis Alison, a Presbyterian minister who had served as the tutor of the revolutionary essayist John Dickinson. A graduate of the College of Philadephia (later the University of Pennsylvania), he joined the common council of Philadelphia at the age of thirty-four. He was a delegate to his state constitutional convention in 1776. During the Revolutionary War, he commanded one of four Philadelphia companies known as the Greens, and eventually rose to the rank of colonel in the Fourth Pennsylvania Line. He was taken prisoner during the effort to defend Fort Washington on the Hudson River. After resigning his commission, Cadwalader entered politics, serving as a member of the Confederation Congress from 1785 to 1787. He was elected to the First Federal Congress as well as the Third, in both cases as a proadministration representative. Cadwalader was a gracious host at his New Jersey estate, Greenwood, where George Washington was a frequent guest.

CARROLL, DANIEL (1730–1796)

Representative from Maryland; Federalist

A member of one of the leading Catholic families of Maryland, Carroll was educated at the Jesuit School at Bohemia, Maryland, and later at the College of St. Omer in France, the same Jesuit college attended by Aedanus Burke. Carroll was a member of the Continental Congress that signed the Articles of Confederation and then a member of the Confederation Congress after it began its first session in 1781. He was a delegate to the Philadelphia convention in 1787 although illness kept him from attending its earliest sessions. William Pierce, a fellow delegate, declared that Carroll "possesses plain good sense, and is in the full confidence of his Countrymen." He was until his death a member of the Maryland senate. During the ratification battles in Maryland, he defended the Constitution against attacks by Antifederalist Samuel Chase, publishing several essays in the *Maryland Journal.* At fifty-nine, he was one of the oldest members elected to the First Federal Congress. During his term, he was active in the debates over the location of the federal capital, and President Washington appointed him one of the commissioners to locate the District of Columbia. After leaving service in the federal government in 1795, Carroll returned to his role as a gentleman farmer. In the last year of his life, however, he became one of George Washington's partners in the Patowmack Company, an enterprise to create a canal linking the middle states with the growing western settlements.

CLYMER, GEORGE (1739–1813)
Representative from Pennsylvania; Federalist

Clymer's father emigrated to Philadelphia from Bristol, England. He died when Clymer was only seven years old, and Clymer was raised by his maternal uncle, William Coleman. Coleman saw to his education, took him into his business, and eventually left him the bulk of his own fortune. Clymer played an active role in prerevolutionary politics and was a signer of the Declaration of Independence in 1776. When war began, he was chosen as captain of a volunteer battalion called the Pennsylvania Silk Stockings, a name suggestive of the social status of its members. Although the battalion never actually saw military action, Clymer did suffer personal losses when his home was plundered by the British army. At the end of the war, Clymer moved to Princeton and was elected to the Pennsylvania legislature, where he helped reform the state criminal code. In 1787, he was a delegate to the Philadelphia Convention, and following ratification of the Constitution, he was elected as a proadministration member of the First Federal Congress at the age of fifty. He did not stand for reelection in 1790. In 1791, he was appointed a collector of excise duties, but he resigned in the wake of Pennsylvania's Whiskey Rebellion. Clymer, said to be modest and unassuming despite his wealth, was a handsome man with a lifelong interest in science and literature. His eulogist declared Clymer's predominant passion to be the promotion of every scheme for the improvement of his country.

COLES, ISAAC (1747–1813)
Representative from Virginia; Antifederalist

Coles, a Virginia planter, received his education at the College of William and Mary. During the Revolutionary War, he saw service as a colonel of the

Virginia militia. He first held political office at the age of thirty-three, when he was elected to the Virginia house of delegates in 1780. He was a delegate to the state ratifying convention and voted against the Constitution, which he believed had "poison under its wings." Coles was a planter, but he voted to abolish slavery, something his brother-in-law Antifederalist leader Elbridge Gerry of Massachusetts would not do. At the age of forty-two Coles was elected to the First Federal Congress as an Antifederalist; he also served in the Third and Fourth Congresses. He was defeated in 1797 in his bid for a return to Congress by an opponent who claimed Coles was unfit because he had married an Englishwoman rather than a Virginian. Coles was described by the historian of his county, Pittsylvania, as a man of generous hospitality and keen wit who entertained his guests with anecdotes from his full and active life.

CONTEE, BENJAMIN (1755–1815)
Representative from Maryland; Antifederalist

Contee was born at Brookefield, a family estate in Prince Georges County, Maryland, and attended a private school though not a college. During the American Revolution, he served as a lieutenant and a captain in the Third Maryland Battalion. He was elected to the state house of delegates in 1785 and served until 1787. In 1788 he was in the Confederation Congress and the following year, at the age of thirty-four, he took his seat in the First Federal Congress. He did not stand for a second term. Contee traveled widely in Europe and studied theology both abroad and in the United States. He was ordained as a minister of the Episcopal Church in Charles County, Maryland, in 1803. He was narrowly defeated in an election to be Episcopal bishop of Maryland in 1814. On June 12, 1789, Contee wrote to a friend, "I esteem it a real truth that the Govt. is a Govt. of the people."

FITZSIMONS, THOMAS (1741–1811)
Representative from Pennsylvania; Federalist

Thomas Fitzsimons was born in Ireland and immigrated to Pennsylvania sometime in the 1750s or 1760s. He entered a countinghouse in Philadelphia as a clerk and rose to be a leading merchant of that city. His firm traded in the West Indies for four decades. He was one of the founders of the Bank of North America and a director of the Insurance Company of North America. Proud of his Irish heritage, Fitzsimons became a member of the Friendly Sons of St. Patrick in 1771. He commanded a volunteer home guard during the Revolutionary War, and later in the war he served as head of a board to oversee the newly formed Pennsylvania navy. As evidence of his support for independence, he donated £5,000 to the Continental Army. Fitzsimons sat in the Confederation Congress in 1782 and 1783. He served in his state house of representatives in 1786 and 1787 and was a delegate to the Philadelphia convention. With Daniel Carroll, he was one of two Catholics to sign the Constitution. He was elected to the First Federal Congress at the age of forty-eight and served in Congress through its third session, which ended in 1795. He failed in his bid for election to the Fourth Congress. Fitzsimons was a philanthropist and served as a trustee of the University of Pennsylvania and participated in the founding of the College of Georgetown. His sense of civic responsibility can be seen in his statement: "I conceive it to be a duty to contend for what is right, be the issue as it may." At his death, a contemporary observed that Fitzsimons died "in the esteem, affection and gratitude of all classes of his fellow citizens."

FLOYD, WILLIAM (1734–1821)

Representative from New York; Antifederalist

Floyd, who as a teenager inherited a large estate from his father, received little formal education. During the Revolutionary War, he served as a major general of the state militia and was a member of the Continental Congress from 1774 to 1776. He was a signer of the Declaration of Independence. Floyd was apparently taciturn; South Carolina's Edmund Rutledge, who served with him in the Continental Congress, placed him among the "good men who never quit their chairs." But if Floyd rarely rose to speak, he attended with regularity and voted on most issues. He was sent at the age of fifty-five to the First Federal Congress, where he was one of the older members of the House, but he was not reelected for the Second Congress. He ran for but did not win election to the New York lieutenant governorship in 1795, but did serve in state government in the early nineteenth century. In his eulogy, the Reverend Charles A. Goodrich described Floyd as a man who "appeared to enjoy the pleasures of private life, yet in his manners he was less familiar, and in his disposition less affable, than most men." However, Goodrich added, Floyd's judgment was respected, his firmness and resolution were admirable, and he was a man of great candor and sincerity.

FOSTER, ABIEL (1735–1806)

Representative from New Hampshire; Federalist

Born in Massachusetts, Foster was a graduate of Harvard College, where he studied theology. He was ordained as pastor in Canterbury, New Hampshire, in 1761 and served in that capacity until 1779. He was a member of the Confederation Congress from 1783 to 1785 and a judge, and later chief justice, of the court of common pleas of Rockingham County from 1784 to 1788. He served in the First Federal Congress, entering at the age of fifty-five, and later in the Fourth through the Seventh Congresses.

GALE, GEORGE (1756–1815)
Representative from Maryland; Federalist

Gale attended the common schools of Somerset County, Maryland, and the College of New Jersey (Princeton). He served in the Continental Army during the Revolution. Gale was a member of the Maryland ratifying convention in 1788, and the following year, at the age of thirty-three, entered the First Federal Congress. In 1791, President Washington appointed him supervisor of distilled liquors for the district of Maryland.

GERRY, ELBRIDGE (1744–1814)
Representative from Massachusetts; Antifederalist

Gerry, a graduate of Harvard College, intended to study medicine but was drawn instead into his father's mercantile business. The family fortune was based on the exporting of codfish to Barbados and Spain and it was lucrative enough that Gerry was soon able to devote most of his attention to politics. Before he was thirty, he was already a member of the Massachusetts legislature and, despite his youthfulness, he took a leading part in its debates. It was Gerry who proposed that the local government outfit armed vessels and establish a court of admiralty. Gerry was offered a position as a maritime judge, but he declined it. He took his seat in the Continental Congress on February 6, 1776, and continued to serve in that body and in the Confederation Congress until 1785. He was a delegate to the Philadelphia convention and was one the few men attending who refused to sign the Constitution. William Pierce was not impressed with Gerry's oratorical skills, calling him a "hesitating and laborious speaker." Although Gerry later gave the new government his support, he remained a critic of the Federalist Party in power during his term in the First and Second Federal Congresses. In 1797 he was sent on a diplomatic mission to France, assigned along with two other American leaders to find a way to preserve peace between it and the United States. In 1798 he ran for governor of his home state and lost; he ran again, without success, in 1801. It was not until 1810, in a heated contest, that he won the governorship, but he lost it in 1812. That same year, he was elected vice president on a ticket with his former political enemy, James Madison, the two men having become allies in the Jeffersonian Party. Thin, with sharp features, the acerbic and brilliant Gerry was reputed to have antagonized nearly everyone. A colleague remarked that Gerry "objected to everything he did not propose." He was inconsistent in his political views and unpredictable; the result was that he often frustrated his allies as much as he irritated his foes. Gerry is best known today for his redistricting plan, which divided political districts in a way that gave his party a distinct advantage in elections, a tactic that came to be known as "gerrymandering."

GILMAN, NICHOLAS (1755–1814)
Representative from New Hampshire; Federalist

Gilman worked at his father's general store before entering the military as a captain in the Continental Army. He returned to run the family business in 1783 but devoted most of his energies in the following years to politics. He served in the Confederation Congress and then as a delegate to the Philadelphia Convention, where he was one of just three bachelors. Although that convention began in May 1787, Gilman did not take his seat until July 21. He was, William Pierce noted, "modest, genteel, and sensible," with nothing brilliant or striking in his character, which perhaps explains why Gilman made no speeches during his weeks at the convention and played only a small role in its deliberations. He believed that the Constitution was "the best that could meet the unanimous concurrence of the States" at the convention. Despite its imperfections, he added, it was the best hope for the new republic to become a respectable nation. He was elected to the First Federal Congress at the age of thirty-four as a Federalist but later shifted his loyalty to the Jeffersonian Party. He served in the first four Congresses, finally declining to run for reelection in 1796. He became a senator in 1805 and served until his death in 1814.

GOODHUE, BENJAMIN (1748–1814)
Representative from Massachusetts; Federalist

A merchant and a graduate of Harvard College, Goodhue was forty-one when he was elected to the First Federal Congress. He served in the three following Congresses until he resigned in June 1796. He was sent to the Senate that year to fill a vacancy caused by the resignation of George Cabot. He sat in the Senate until 1800. Goodhue's dislike of his fellow Massachusetts representative Elbridge Gerry was captured in a letter to a friend on August 11, 1789. Gerry, he wrote, "manifested such an illiberal and ugly a disposition since he has been in Congress that I believe no man has fewer friends than Mr. Gerry." [1]

GRIFFIN, SAMUEL (1746–1810)
Representative from Virginia; Federalist

Griffin was educated privately and, after studying law, was admitted to the Virginia bar. During the Revolutionary War, he served as a colonel and as an aide-de-camp to General Charles Lee. He was wounded soon after the war officially began, in the Battle of Harlem Heights on September 16, 1776. In

1786, he was elected to a seat in the Virginia house of delegates, a position he held until 1788. He was elected to the First Federal Congress at the age of forty-three as a Federalist but in the next Congress he served as an antiadministration member. In the Third Congress he was once again a supporter of the administration. Gilbert Stuart's portrait of Griffin, painted the year he died at age sixty-four, shows a man with curly gray hair and a cheerful face. Griffin was said to be "inattentive to Business,"and "too fond of Pleasure" but he was regular in his attendance while a congressman.[2]

GROUT, JONATHAN (1737–1807)
Representative from Massachusetts; Antifederalist

Born in Worcester County, Massachusetts, Grout served in the ill-fated British expedition against Canada during the French and Indian War and would see military service again, fighting this time against the British, in the Revolutionary War. Grout practiced law in Petersham, Massachuetts, and entered politics with his election to the state house of representatives in 1781. He was a member of the state ratifying convention, where he opposed the Constitution, and was then elected to the First Federal Congress as an Antifederalist. He served until the end of that Congress, when he returned to Lunenburg, Massachusetts (now a town in Vermont).

HARTLEY, THOMAS (1748–1800)
Representative from Pennsylvania; Federalist

Hartley studied law and established a practice in York, Pennsylvania, in 1789. He served in the Revolutionary War as a colonel of the Sixth Pennsylvania Regiment in 1776 and commanded an expedition against Indians involved in what was known as the Wyoming Massacre of 1778. He was a member of his state ratifying convention, where he voted for the Constitution, and was elected at the age of forty-one as a Federalist to the First Federal Congress; he was also elected to the Second through the Sixth, until his death in 1800. At a dinner given in his honor before he left for the Federal Congress in 1789, Hartley commented: "My abilities, I well know, are not of the superior kind, but it will be my study to do what is right; and with the assistance of abler counsel, I trust that religion and learning, as well as the rights of human kind, will be advanced and protected under the new government." [3]

HATHORN, JOHN (1749–1825)
Representative from New York; Antifederalist

Born in Wilmington, Delaware, Hathorn was a surveyor and a schoolteacher who settled in Warwick, New York, where he had established himself as a merchant, an investor in iron manufacturing, a landowner, and the town's tax assessor. Throughout the Revolutionary War he was a colonel of the Fourth Orange County (New York) Regiment, and he rose to the rank of brigadier general of the Orange County Militia in 1786. In 1778 he was a member of the committee that oversaw the placing of a chain across the Hudson River to obstruct its navigation by enemy ships. He was a member of the state assembly for several terms beginning in 1778, and served as its speaker in 1783 and 1784. He also served in the state senate from 1786 to 1790 and again from 1799 to 1803. He was forty when he and Jeremiah Van Rensselaer were elected the only two Antifederalists from New York in the First Federal Congress. Hathorn was a Quaker, the father of eleven children, and a friend of the Marquis de Lafayette. His years of public service left him impoverished and it is reported that, in 1824, he turned down an invitation to dinner from the marquis because his clothes were too tattered for such a social event. At the age of seventy-three, Hawthorn participated in the dedication of a monument to the militiamen who lost their lives at the Battle of Minisink. In his speech he noted that "monuments to the brave are mementos to their descendants; the honors they record are stars to the patriot in the path of glory."[4]

HIESTER, DANIEL (1747–1804)
Representative from Pennsylvania; Antifederalist

Hiester, whose father emigrated to Pennsylvania from Silesia in 1737, attended public schools before becoming a businessman in Pennsylvania's Montgomery County. He was a colonel and then a brigadier general of the militia and served in the Revolutionary War. Hiester was a member of the supreme council of Pennsylvania from 1784 to 1786, and was elected to the First Federal Congress at the age of forty-two. He served in the Second, Third, and Fourth Congresses as well. He moved to Hagerstown, Maryland, in 1796 and was chosen to represent that state in the Seventh and Eighth Congresses.

HUGER, DANIEL (1742–1799)
Representative from South Carolina; Federalist

One of only two Federalists from his state in the First Federal Congress, Daniel Huger was born on Limerick plantation in Berkeley County, South Carolina. He was the grandson of a French Huguenot who had immigrated to the British colonies. He was educated at home and in schools in Charleston and later he studied in England. When he entered his thirties, Huger became a member of the colonial assembly, and after independence was declared, he served in the state house of representatives and the governor's council. He was a member of the last sessions of the Confederation Congress, from 1786 to 1788, and then was elected to both the First and the Second Federal Congresses. He left national office in 1793 and retired to his plantation, Wateree, devoting his energies to the management of his extensive landholdings. Pierce Butler, a fellow South Carolina political leader, described Huger unfavorably as "a quarrelsome character who had shot Charles Cotesworth Pinckney in the leg in a 1785 duel."

HUNTINGTON, BENJAMIN (1736–1800)
Representative from Connecticut; Federalist

Huntington, an only child and a descendant of a Puritan immigrant to New England, graduated from Yale College in 1761 and, after a brief stint as surveyor of lands for Windham County, Connecticut, he was admitted to the bar and established a practice in his hometown, Norwich. In 1771 he was elected a member of the state house of representatives, a position he held until 1780. He served in the Continental Congress and Confederation Congress and then, at the age of fifty-three, was elected to the First Federal Congress. Huntington was the mayor of Norwich from 1784 until 1796 and a justice of the superior court of Connecticut from 1793 until 1798. Writing to his wife in September 1783 Huntington expressed his hope "to become a small man in a few Weeks and Retire from the Embarrassments of Dignity to the Plain & Peaceful Possessions of a Private Life."[5] Nevertheless he continued to serve in national office for a decade more and remained active in local politics for several years after he left the Federal Congress.

JACKSON, JAMES (1757–1806)
Representative from Georgia; Antifederalist

Jackson immigrated to Georgia from his native Devonshire, England, in 1772. He settled in Savannah, where he established a very lucrative law practice and was a planter. During the Revolution he served in the Georgia state militia, and was wounded in action. He played an active role in the unsuccessful defense of Savannah against the British. He was frequently elected to the state legislature and in 1788 was elected governor, a position he declined. At age thirty-two, he was a representative in the First Federal Congress. He contested the election of military hero Anthony Wayne to a seat in the Second Congress; as a result the seat was declared vacant for the session. In 1793, Jackson entered the Senate, but he resigned in 1795. He accepted the governorship of Georgia in 1798 and served until 1801, when he returned to the Senate as a member of the Jeffersonian Party. Jackson had a much deserved reputation as a fierce-tempered man; he engaged in several duels, killing his opponent in 1780, and was known to participate in street brawls. His biographer, who described Jackson as "a fiery little man," noted his "Turbulent personality, with no inhibitions about displaying his militant disposition on the dueling field or in legislative halls." Jackson's contemporary Catharine Greene, widow of General Nathanael Greene, noted that he was "an honest Man but has a very hot head." [6]

LAURANCE, JOHN (1750–1810)
Representative from New York, Federalist

Laurance, born in Falmouth, England, immigrated to the colonies in 1767 and settled in New York City. Admitted to the bar in 1772, he established his practice in his adopted city and later also engaged in land speculation. During the Revolution, he served as an officer, and, as the judge advocate general, Laurance presided at the trial of a British spy, Major John André. Along with Henry Knox and George Washington, Laurance was a charter member of the Society of the Cincinnati. Laurance was a delegate to the Confederation Congress from 1785 to 1787. Although he presented the application for a second constitutional convention to the New York state legislature, he opposed any structural changes to the Constitution. and was chosen to represent New York in the First Federal Congress at the age of thirty-nine. He served in the Second Congress as well. As a close friend and ally of Alexander Hamilton, Laurance was a vigorous and eloquent defender of Federalist programs and policies. He was elected to the Senate in 1796 and served until August 1800. Laurance married the daughter of the radical Alexander McDougall, a leader of the Sons of Liberty known as the "John Wilkes of America."

LEE, RICHARD BLAND (1761–1827)
Representative from Virginia; Federalist

The younger brother of "Lighthorse Harry" Lee and father of General Robert E. Lee, Richard Bland Lee was born at Leesylvania, an estate in Prince William County, Virginia. He attended the College of William and Mary before entering the state house of delegates in 1784. He strongly opposed Patrick Henry's call for a second constitutional convention during the ratification debates. Lee was elected as a pro-administration member of the First Federal Congress at the age of twenty-eight, making him one of the youngest representatives in the House. George Washington recorded in his diary that he traveled to Alexandria to vote for Lee in this election. Lee also served in the Second and Third Congresses but was defeated in his bid for reelection to the Fourth. He returned to state office, serving in the house of delegates in 1796 and again from 1799 to 1806. He moved from Virginia to Washington, D.C., around

1815. His home in Virginia, called Sully, has been preserved, and one of his family's favorite pets, a white squirrel, was stuffed and can be seen in the parlor of Sully House today.

LEONARD, GEORGE (1729–1819)
Representative from Massachusetts; Federalist

A graduate of Harvard College, Leonard practiced law in his hometown, Norton, Massachusetts. He was a member of the provincial assembly from 1764 to 1766 and a member of the governor's council from 1770 to 1775. In 1798, he was appointed chief justice of the state, a position he held until 1804. At the age of sixty he was elected to the First Federal Congress and served in the Second and Fourth Congresses as well. Although Leonard came from a distinguished family, active in Massachusetts politics, little information about him is available.

LIVERMORE, SAMUEL (1732–1803)
Representative from New Hampshire; Federalist

A graduate of the College of New Jersey (later Princeton), Livermore was admitted to the bar in 1756 and opened his practice in Waltham, Massachusetts. Two years later, he moved to Portsmouth, New Hampshire, and later he moved to Londonderry. He served in the colonial assembly from 1768 to 1769 and was a judge advocate in the admiralty court and colonial attorney general from 1769 to 1774. In 1775, he moved once again, this time to Holderness, New Hampshire, and here he farmed and ran a gristmill. He eventually owned half of the property in the town. Livermore was a member of the Confederation Congress and a delegate to the state ratifying convention in

1788. He entered the First Federal Congress at the age of fifty-seven and also served in the Second Congress. Livermore voted against the judiciary bill; in his argument against it, reported in the *Gazette of the United States*, he warned, "This new fangled system will eventually swallow up the State Courts." He became a senator in 1792 and again in 1793. Ill health forced him to resign his seat in 1801.

MADISON, JAMES (1751–1836)
Representative from Virginia; Federalist

Madison attended the College of New Jersey (now Princeton), where his delicate constitution often caused him to be ill. Despite the college president's insistence that young Jemmy never said or did an indiscreet thing, Madison did write a number of ribald pieces of doggerel poetry. He formed lasting friendships with a group of fellow students including the poet Philip Freneau and the novelist Hugh Henry Brackenridge. He was greatly influenced by the president of the college, John Witherspoon, and might have become a minister had his voice not been both low and thin. Back home in Virginia, Madison did not pursue a law career, despite having studied the subject. Instead he pursued a career in politics. In 1776, at the age of twenty-five he was elected to the Virginia assembly, where he and his friend Thomas Jefferson were instrumental in the passage of the Virginia Bill for Establishing Religious Freedom. He was one of the leading figures of the Philadelphia convention, and his Virginia Plan served as the starting point for the debates that led to the Constitution. With Alexander Hamilton and John Jay, he wrote *The Federalist Papers*, a series of essays that influenced many to support ratification of the Constitution. To acknowledge his efforts on behalf of the new Constitution, the College of New Jersey awarded him an honorary doctor of law degree. Madison was elected to the First Federal Congress at the age of thirty-eight and here he introduced and shepherded through the Congress what would become known as the Bill of Rights. A nationalist at the Philadelphia convention and in the First Congress, he later abandoned that party as a result of Hamilton's economic and fiscal policies and helped Jefferson create a new opposition party. In 1798 he drafted the Virginia Resolutions, a nullification of the Adams administration's Alien and Sedition Acts. When Jefferson became president in 1801, Madison served as his secretary of state. In 1809, Madison became the fourth president of the United States; he served two terms, during which the War of 1812 was fought. He retired to his estate, Montpelier, after his presidency. Short and somewhat awkward with women, Madison did not marry until he was forty-three years old. His wife, the beautiful Dolley Payne Todd, was one of the capital's most influential hostesses. Of Madison, Jefferson would say: "I do not know in the world a man of purer integrity, more dispassionate, disinterested, and devoted to Republicanism, nor could I in the whole scope of America and Europe point out an abler head."

MATHEWS, GEORGE (1739–1812)
Representative from Georgia; Antifederalist

Mathews, son of Irish and Welsh immigrants, was born in Virginia and served in the Virginia militia in the French and Indian War as well as the Revolutionary War. He was a war hero, said to have been stabbed five to seven times at the Battle of Brandywine. He was captured at Germantown in 1777 and held prisoner until December 1781. In partnership with his brother Sampson, Mathews ran successful agricultural and mercantile enterprises and became a land speculator. He moved to Georgia, possibly in 1785, and he began a new life there, living at first in a log cabin with his family. By 1787, he had become governor of Georgia, a position he held again from 1793 to 1796. He was fifty years old when he was elected to the First Federal Congress. Implicated in a scandal called the Yazoo Land Fraud, Mathews retired from politics, relocating to the Mississippi Territory. In 1811, he was one of the leaders of a revolt against the Spanish government's control of East Florida.

MOORE, ANDREW (1752–1821)
Representative from Virginia; Federalist

Moore was born at Cannicello, an estate south of Staunton, Virginia, the son of Scotch-Irish parents. He attended Augusta Academy (now Washington and Lee College) and studied law. Legend has it that, during his college years, Moore traveled to the West Indies, was shipwrecked, and lived with his fellow castaways on a diet of lizards until they were rescued. Moore was a captain in the Revolutionary War, and was with the Americans who defeated Burgoyne at Saratoga. At the Virginia ratifying convention, he voted for the Constitution, and he was elected to the First Federal Congress at the age of thirty-seven. He served in the three succeeding Congresses, becoming increasingly critical of the Federalist policies put forward by Alexander Hamilton. He was appointed to the Senate as a member of the Jeffersonian Party in 1804. He served in the Senate for two terms. Moore was a large man, who, like other gentlemen of his day, wore knee pants, ruffled sleeves, buckles on his shoes, and silk stockings.

MUHLENBERG, FREDERICK AUGUSTUS CONRAD (1750–1801)
Representative from Pennsylvania; Federalist

Muhlenberg was the son of a German immigrant who was a renowned Lutheran minister. He attended the University of Halle, Germany, where he studied theology, and was ordained a minister of the Lutheran Church in Pennsylvania in 1770. He preached in Pennsylvania and, from 1774 through

1776, in New York City. When the British occupied that city, he returned to Pennsylvania. He was a member of the Pennsylvania house of representatives from 1780 to 1783 and a delegate to the state ratifying convention in 1787. At his election to the First Federal Congress, Muhlenberg was a thirty-nine-year-old Federalist; when elected to the Second and Third Congresses, he was an antiadministration member; by the Fourth Congress, he was a member of the Jeffersonian Party. A magazine described him as a man with powdered hair, a "sonorous voice," and a "rubicund complexion and oval face." On Muhlenberg's death, the Pennsylvania political leader William Duane wrote to Thomas Jefferson, "There is no other character among the Germans of the talents and standing of the deceased."

MUHLENBERG, JOHN PETER GABRIEL (1746–1807)
Representative from Pennsylvania; Antifederalist

Muhlenberg was the older brother of Frederick Muhlenberg and, like his brother, he studied at the University of Halle. There, his mentors recommended that he enter commerce rather than the Lutheran ministry, for he seemed to prefer fishing to studying. He was apprenticed to a merchant in Lübeck who mistreated him and he ran away, joining the Royal American Regiment of Foot of the British army. He returned to Philadelphia as secretary to one of the regiment officers and received an honorable discharge in 1767. He then prepared for the ministry and won acclaim as a preacher. He was called to a church in Virginia, and while there, he became a follower of Patrick Henry. When the Revolution began, Muhlenberg gave up his ministerial position to join the military. Legend has it that in the course of his final sermon he declared, "There is a time to pray and a time to fight, and that time has now come." He then enlisted in the Continental Army, achieving the rank of major general. He participated in the battle at Charleston in

1776 and in the battles of Brandywine, Germantown, and Monmouth, and he was at Yorktown when General Cornwallis surrendered. After the war, Muhlenberg returned to Pennsylvania but not to the pulpit. He entered politics, was elected a member of the state council, and in 1785 was chosen to be vice president of Pennsylvania. He was forty-three when he went to the First Federal Congress and he later served in the Third and the Sixth Congresses. In March 1801, he became a senator, but he resigned on June 30 of that year in order to take a lucrative appointment as collector of customs of the port of Philadelphia.

PAGE, JOHN (1743–1808)
Representative from Virginia; Antifederalist

Page graduated from the College of William and Mary in 1763. He served under fellow Virginian George Washington in an expedition against the French and Indians in the French and Indian War and served as an officer of the Virginia state militia during the American Revolution. In 1776, he was a member of the convention that created the constitution of the new state of Virginia, and he became the state's lieutenant governor from 1776 to 1779. At the age of forty-six, he was elected as a representative to the First Federal Congress. He would hold this office again in the following three Congresses. He became governor of Virginia in 1802 and held that position until 1805. Page was married to Margaret Lowther Page, a poet who held a salon at their plantation, Rosewell. Her husband also tried his hand at writing poetry, composing a long poem about national political issues such as the farmers' revolt in Massachusetts known as Shays's Rebellion. Page has the distinction of being quoted by President George W. Bush in his inaugural address of 2001.

PARKER, JOSIAH (1751–1810)

Representative from Virginia; Antifederalist

At the age of twenty-three, Parker was one of the founding members of the revolutionary committee in his home county, Isle of Wight. During the Revolutionary War, he served heroically, leading Virginia's Fifth Regiment at the capture of Trenton, where he was chosen to receive the sword of surrender from the defeated Hessian commander. He won acclaim for his bravery at Brandywine as well. Parker is shown directly behind General George Washington in Emanuel Leutze's famous painting *Washington Crossing the Delaware*. After leaving military service he was elected to the Virginia house of delegates in 1778, 1779, 1782, and 1783. He was elected to the First Federal Congress at the age of thirty-eight and served two terms as an Antifederalist representative but the next four terms as a Federalist. Parker inherited 398 acres of land and a number of slaves but opposed slavery and urged Congress to put an end to it.

PARTRIDGE, GEORGE (1740–1828)

Representative from Massachusetts; Federalist

Partridge was a graduate of Harvard College and for several years a teacher at Kingston, Massachusetts. Although he studied theology, he was never ordained. He became a member of the provincial congress in 1774 and a member of the state house of representatives in 1775. He served in the Continental and Confederation Congresses from 1779 until 1785. At the age of forty-nine, he became a member of the First Federal Congress, although he resigned in August 1790. He retired to the large farm he had inherited from an uncle. Partridge bequeathed a major portion of his estate for religious and educational usc. His contribution made it possible ultimately to create Partridge Academy in Duxbury in 1844. In his eulogy, Benjamin Kent described Partridge as a man whose spirit was as "humble as it was philanthropic, as unostentatious as it was gentle and dignified."

SCHUREMAN, JAMES (1756–1824)
Representative from New Jersey; Federalist

A member of the Dutch Reformed Church, Schureman graduated from Queen's College (now Rutgers University) and became a merchant. During the Revolution, he led a volunteer company that took part in the Battle of Long Island. He was taken prisoner, but managed to escape. He rejoined the army at Morristown. He sat in his state's general assembly from 1783 to 1785 and was a delegate to the Confederation Congress in 1786 and 1787. He was thirty-three when he was elected to the First Federal Congress. Schureman was elected once again to the Fifth Congress and following that, he was appointed to fill a vacancy in the Senate. After leaving national office, he served as mayor of New Brunswick until his death. Schureman owned a farm, and his interest in agriculture prompted him to help establish the New Jersey Agricultural Society. Schureman reportedly saved the life of a Loyalist officer, Lieutenant Colonel John Simcoe, during the war by preventing a militiaman from bayoneting him while he lay unconscious.[7]

SCOTT, THOMAS (1739–1796)
Representative from Pennsylvania; Federalist

Of Scottish background, Scott attended school in rural Pennsylvania and later studied law. He was a member of the first Pennsylvania assembly in 1776 and a member of the state's supreme council the following year. He was elected to the First Federal Congress at the age of fifty but declined to stand for reelection in 1790. He did agree to serve in the Third Congress, however. Scott was said to have presented the resolution that established the new capital city on the banks of the Potomac River.[8]

SEDGWICK, THEODORE (1746–1813)

Representative from Massachusetts; Federalist

Born in Connecticut, Sedgwick was the son of a merchant who died when Sedgwick was thirteen years old. He attended Yale College but did not graduate. He was admitted to the bar in 1766 and set up his practice in Great Barrington, Massachusetts. He later moved to Sheffield. During the Revolutionary War, Sedgwick served in the failed expedition against Canada. He was a member of the Massachusetts house of representatives and its senate and represented his state in the Confederation Congress in 1785, 1786, and 1788. He was a delegate to the state ratifying convention and, at the age of forty-three, chosen as a representative to the First Federal Congress. He served in four consecutive Congresses. He resigned his seat in 1796 in order to fill a vacancy in the Senate. He returned to the House for the Sixth Congress. He became a judge of the supreme court of Massachusetts in 1802 and remained on the bench until his death in 1813. Sedgwick is best remembered as the young lawyer who in 1781, along with Tapping Reeve, pleaded the case of *Brom and Bett v. Ashley*, often called the "freedom suit." Brom and Bett were slaves of Colonel John Ashley, and Bett had run away because of cruel treatment by her master. The attorneys argued that the new state constitution declared all men free and equal and thus the two African Americans deserved their freedom. The jury agreed. Bett then took the name Elizabeth Freeman and was employed by the Sedgwick family. She was buried in the Sedgwick family cemetery. Sedgwick was also instrumental in crushing the farmers' revolt known as Shays's Rebellion.

SENEY, JOSHUA (1756–1798)
Representative from Maryland; Antifederalist

A descendant of Huguenot immigrants, Seney was born in Queen Annes County, Maryland, and graduated from the College of Philadelphia (later the University of Pennsylvania) and became a lawyer and a farmer. He was a member of the Maryland house of delegates from 1785 to 1787, at the same time as his father, and served in the First and Second Federal Congresses, beginning at the age of thirty-three. He became chief justice of the third judicial district of Maryland in 1792. In 1798 he was elected to Congress as a Jeffersonian, but he died before taking office.

SHERMAN, ROGER (1721–1793)
Representative from Connecticut; Federalist

Sherman began his career as a shoemaker. When his father died in 1741, he became responsible for the support of his mother and several younger siblings. In 1743, he moved the family to New Milford, and soon afterward he went into business with a brother, keeping a small store. Throughout this period, Sherman studied mathematics and educated himself with the help of his late father's library and the assistance of a local minister. In 1745, he was appointed the surveyor for New Haven County. Although he had no legal training, he was admitted to the bar in 1754, and entered political life the following year with his election to the Connecticut assembly. He moved to New Haven in 1761, and by 1766 was a member of the colonial senate and judge of the superior court. As a delegate to the Continental Congress from 1774 to 1781, Sherman served on the committee to draft the Declaration of Independence. He was the only person to sign three major state papers of the era: the Declaration of Independence, the Articles of Confederation, and the Constitution. He was chosen mayor of New Haven, a position he held until his death. Sherman was a delegate to the Philadelphia convention and was elected at the age of sixty-eight to the First Federal Congress, where he was the oldest representative. He became a senator in 1791 and remained in the Senate until his death in 1793. Sherman was widely respected by Federalists and Antifederalists alike. Although William Pierce found him "awkward, unmeaning, and unaccountably strange in his manner," he conceded that "he deserves infinite praise" for his good heart and clear head. Jeremiah Wadsworth said of him that "he is not easily managed, but if he suspects you are trying to take him in, you may as well catch an Eel by the tail." And Thomas Jefferson observed that Roger Sherman had "never said a foolish thing in his life."

SILVESTER, PETER (1734–1808)

Representative from New York; Federalist

Silvester is believed to have been born on Shelter Island, New York. He was admitted to the bar in 1755; the following year he was made a 'free man" of Albany, a status that allowed him to conduct business in that city. As a lawyer in Albany, Silvester counted Sir William Johnson, the commissioner of Indian Affairs, among his clients. He was elected to serve on the Albany Committee of Correspondence in 1775 and soon joined the New York Provincial Congress. In the 1770s, Silvester moved his family to Kinderhook, where his wife had inherited land, although he continued to practice law in Albany. Although his wife's family, the Van Schaacks, were not supporters of the Revolution, Silvester's patriotism was not questioned and he was elected to the First Federal Congress at the age of fifty-five. After serving in two Congresses, he returned to local politics, becoming a member of the state senate and then the state assembly.

SINNICKSON, THOMAS (1744–1817)
Representative from New Jersey; Federalist

Sinnickson, a merchant of Scandinavian descent, served as a captain in the Revolutionary War and saw action in the battles of Trenton and Princeton. He served in the New Jersey general assembly in 1777 and again throughout the 1780s. He was forty-five when elected to the First Federal Congress, and he served a second term in the Fifth Congress. His pro-independence writings were said to have led British commander Lord Howe to offer a "Dead or Alive" bounty on Sinnickson's head.

SMITH, WILLIAM (1728–1814)
Representative from Maryland; Antifederalist

Smith, a merchant, was born in Lancaster County, Pennsylvania, but moved to Baltimore at the age of thirty-three. Here he was appointed a member of the Maryland committee of correspondence in 1774. In 1775 he was one of the residents of Harford Town (then called Bush) who signed a declaration pledging support for resistance against Britain "at the risqué of our lives and fortunes." He was a member of the Continental Congress in 1777 and was elected to the First Federal Congress at the age of sixty-one: along with Roger Sherman, he was one of the oldest members of that body. He was named first auditor of the United States Treasury in 1791. He returned to local politics and was a member of the Maryland senate in 1801.

SMITH, WILLIAM LOUGHTON (1758–1812)
Representative from South Carolina; Federalist

Born in Charleston, Smith attended preparatory schools in England and studied law in the Middle Temple at London. He then continued his studies in Geneva, returning at last to Charleston at the end of the Revolutionary War, in 1783. He was both a planter and an attorney. He served in South Carolina's privy council and in its house of representatives before being elected at the age of thirty-one to the First Federal Congress. He was returned to Congress for the second through the fifth sessions. In 1797, Smith was appointed U.S. minister to Portugal and Spain, a position he held until 1801. He was unsuccessful in his bids as a Federalist candidate for the Ninth, Tenth, and Eleventh Congresses. He was the president of the Santee Canal Company and the vice president of the Charleston Library Society. In his public writing, particularly an essay he wrote under the name "Phocion," he was a harsh critic of Thomas Jefferson's administration. Although Alexander Hamilton viewed Smith as "a ready clear speaker, of a sound analytic head, and the justest of views," he hesitated to recommend him to President Washington as secretary of state. He considered Smith a man of industry and integrity but "of an uncomfortable temperament," unpopular with most men because of a "hardness of character." [9]

STONE, MICHAEL JENIFER (1747–1812)
Representative from Maryland; Federalist/Antifederalist

Born on the family plantation, Equality, Stone, a tobacco planter and lawyer, was the younger brother of Thomas Stone, who signed the Declaration of Independence. He entered political life in 1781 as a member of the Maryland house of delegates. He was a member of the Maryland ratifying convention and was elected at the age of forty-two to the First Federal Congress. A supporter of the administration in the beginning of the session, he soon split with the Federalists over the chartering of the Bank of the United States and other Hamiltonian policies.

STURGES, JONATHAN (1740–1819)
Representative from Connecticut; Federalist

A graduate of Yale College, Sturges was admitted to the bar in Connecticut in 1772 and established a practice in Fairfield. He was a member of the Connecticut house of representatives from 1772 to 1784 and a judge of the probate court for the district of Fairfield. He was forty-nine when he was elected to the First Federal Congress, and he served also in the Second Congress. He became a judge of the Connecticut supreme court in 1793 and sat on the bench until 1805.

SUMTER, THOMAS (1734–1832)
Representative from South Carolina; Antifederalist

Sumter was born in Virginia, where, as a young man, he was said to have been devoted to "gambling, cockfighting and horse racing." He had a long and distinguished military career, beginning as a young volunteer in the French and Indian War. During that war, he was with Braddock when the English general was defeated. Later, he fought against the Cherokees. He moved to South Carolina in the early 1760s, after a brief incarceration in a Virginia prison for an unpaid debt. He built a store and purchased land on the Santee River. He served with South Carolina troops throughout the Revolutionary War, beginning as a lieutenant colonel in the Second Regiment of riflemen.

When Charleston fell in May 1780, Sumter took refuge in the local swamps. When his estate was burned and looted, he made his way to North Carolina and raised a large force to fight the British. He routed the enemy in a confrontation at the Catawba River and next attacked them at Rocky Mount. Known as the "Carolina Gamecock," Sumter continued to lead raids until late 1780, when a severe wound in his shoulder sidelined him. He returned to duty in early 1781. He began his political career in 1782, when he was elected to the state privy council, and afterward served several terms in the South Carolina house of representatives. At the state ratifying convention, Sumter voted against the adoption of the Constitution. At the age of fifty-five, he was elected to the First Federal Congress; he served in the Fifth, Sixth, and Seventh as well. He was appointed to the Senate in 1801 and served in that body until his resignation in 1810. He then retired from public life to his plantation, South Mount, where he raised racing horses.

THATCHER, GEORGE (1754–1824)
Representative from Massachusetts; Federalist

Thatcher was born in Yarmouth and graduated from Harvard College in 1776. He was admitted to the bar two years later and began a practice in Maine (then a part of Massachusetts). He was a member of the Confederation Congress from 1787 to its demise in 1789 and that year, at the age of thirty-five, was elected to the First Federal Congress. He served in Congress from 1789 to 1801. When he retired, he was the last of the original congressmen still in office. He served in the Massachusetts government after leaving national office and was appointed to the state supreme judicial court. When Maine was organizing for statehood, he was a member of the convention that drafted its state constitution. Under the name "Scribble Scrabble," Thatcher published an influential political essay in which he defended the Portland Convention, an assembly called by several Maine counties to discuss independence from Massachusetts. He also helped create Bowdoin College in Maine. A contemporary wrote of him: "In domestic relations, he had no fault unless an excess of kindness and indulgence be one. Surrounded by his sons and daughters, and their children, and having the government of his family upon equal terms with a most exemplary and excellent wife, his humble dwelling was the abode of peace, love and benevolence." [10]

TRUMBULL, JONATHAN, JR. (1740–1809)
Representative from Connecticut; Federalist

Trumbull was a graduate of Harvard, and received both his BA and MA from that college. He ran a small store in his hometown, Lebanon, and began his political career on the local level, serving as a surveyor of highways, justice of the peace, and selectman and then, in his early thirties, becoming a member of the colonial and state legislatures of Connecticut. During the Revolutionary War, he served as a paymaster in the Continental Army and in 1781 became the secretary of General George Washington. At the age of forty-nine, he was elected to the First Federal Congress, and he served in the Second and Third as well. He became a senator in 1795 and served until June 1796, when he resigned. He became governor of Connecticut the following year and served eleven consecutive terms. On his election as speaker of the House of the Connecticut assembly, on October 24, 1791, Trumbull declared: "I find my self unable to express to you the full sense I have of the distinguished honor you have done me. . . . I shall endeavor to conduct myself with that impartiality, integrity, and assiduity, which become the conspicuous station in which you have been pleased to place me." His death in 1809 was attributed to "dropsy of the heart."

TUCKER, THOMAS TUDOR (1745–1828)
Representative from South Carolina; Antifederalist

Tucker, born in Port Royal, Bermuda, studied medicine at the University of Edinburgh before moving first to Virginia and then to Charleston, South Carolina. Here, he fell into debt in the early years of his medical practice in large part because Charleston had more doctors than it could comfortably sustain. He lamented, "The Difficulties of getting Bread from day to day are almost insurpassable," and decided that the world "seems to have been intended as a School for Stoicism." It did not help that he became involved in a scandal in 1773, when he was accused of allowing a man infected with smallpox to roam about the city of Charleston. Although he challenged the man who made the accusation in the newspapers to a duel, he did not receive satisfaction; instead, he was sued for libel. In the 1780s he was wounded in another duel, this time with South Carolina political leader Ralph Izard. During the Revolutionary War, Tucker served as a surgeon in a military hospital. After the war, his finances improved and he was respected enough to be elected a member of the state assembly in 1776, 1782–1783, 1785, and 1787–1788. In 1784 he wrote a pamphlet entitled *Conciliatory Hints, Attempting . . . to Remove Party-Prejudices*, which criticized the British form of government and praised democracy. He was forty-four years old when he was elected to the First Federal Congress; he also served in the Second Congress. President Thomas Jefferson appointed him U.S. treasurer in 1801, a position he held until his death in 1828—the longest serving treasurer in the history of the country. While he was treasurer, Tucker also acted as President James Madison's personal physician. Tucker was a man of considerable contradictions: he criticized the gentry but was pleased to be counted among them; in Congress, fellow representatives found him ill-humored, yet he and John Page of Virginia exchanged riddles in verse during House sessions. James Madison declared him a man "truly attached to republican principles, of a very ingenious mind, extensive information, & great exactitude in his ideas . . ."[11]

VAN RENSSELAER, JEREMIAH (1738–1810)
Representative from New York; Antifederalist

A graduate of the College of New Jersey (later Princeton), Van Rensselaer was a land agent, merchant, and surveyor. In the years preceding the revolution, he was a member of the Albany Sons of Liberty and of Albany's committee of safety; during the war he was a paymaster in New York's Third Regiment. He was a member of the Albany city council from 1770 until the war caused the Albany corporation to suspend its operations. He was probably unique among the Van Rensselaers in opposing the ratification of the Constitution. At the age of fifty-one, he was elected to the First Federal Congress, but he lost his bid for reelection to the Second Congress. He served on the first board of directors of the Bank of Albany and later became the bank's president. He was lieutenant governor of New York from 1801 to 1804 and curator of the Evangelical Lutheran Seminary in Albany in 1804.

VINING, JOHN (1758–1802)
Representative from Delaware; Federalist

Vining was the son of a prominent lawyer and landowner who had served as speaker of the colonial assembly and chief justice of Delaware. His godfather was Caesar Rodney, a signer of the Declaration of Independence. Vining's father died when John was eleven years old, leaving the boy and his sister a sizable fortune. Vining, a lawyer, began his political career as a member of the Confederation Congress in 1784. He then served in the Delaware house of assembly for two sessions, beginning in 1787. He was his state's only member of the House in the First Federal Congress, elected at the age of thirty-one. He was reelected for the Second Congress. While in the House, he married the poet Anna Maria Seaton. He next entered the Senate in 1793 and served until 1798. Known as "Jack," Vining was handsome, friendly, and outspoken. Some called him "colorful," a man who "brandished a florid metaphor," but others found him verbose and inclined to use inflammatory language. He ran through his fortune, became an alcoholic, and died impoverished, leaving behind four sons who all died young. A memoirist from Delaware described Vining as a man of "brilliant talents, not nourished by application, withered in the bud. Indolence and generosity engendered extravagance that wasted his substance."

WADSWORTH, JEREMIAH (1743–1804)
Representative from Connecticut; Federalist

Wadsworth, the son of a pastor with the First Church of Christ, went to sea when he was eighteen, and became the first mate and later the captain of a vessel. He was appointed commissary to the revolutionary forces of Connecticut in 1775, and rose to the rank of commissary general in 1778. After the war, he engaged successfully in a variety of businesses, including the shipping industry, and was one of the founders of the Bank of North America and the Hartford Bank. He was described in a history of Hartford as "the wealthiest man in town . . . foremost in every enterprise which promised to advance its prosperity." He attended his state's ratifying convention, voting in favor of the Constitution, and at the age of forty-six was elected to the First Federal Congress. In 1795 he was elected to the Connecticut state legislature and the executive council. He funded the creation of the Wadsworth Atheneum, the nation's oldest public art museum. At his death, he left a huge estate of over six thousand acres in South Carolina, land given to him by his friend General Nathanael Greene in payment for a loan made by Wadsworth. Despite his wealth, Wadsworth avoided any appearance of arrogance. He told his daughter, "If you ever find your Selfe angry or ill-natured shut your selfe up for half an hour which will cure you."[12]

WHITE, ALEXANDER (1738–1804)
Representative from Virginia; Federalist

White was educated at the University of Edinburgh and studied law at the Inner Temple in London. He returned to America in 1765 and established a legal practice in Virginia. He did not serve in the military during the Revolutionary War, but acted as the attorney for Quakers and for Hessian civil prisoners held on suspicion of supporting the British. In 1772 he was elected to the Virginia house of burgesses; after independence, he was a member of the state house of delegates from 1782 to 1786 and again from 1799 to 1801. At the state ratifying convention he voted in favor of the adoption of the Constitution. During the battle over the Constitution, he published political essays as "An Independent Freeholder." President Washington appointed him one of three commissioners to lay out the city of Washington, D.C. White was an eloquent speaker and reportedly very punctual in his attendance in Congress. At his death, he freed his slaves.

WYNKOOP, HENRY (1737–1816)
Representative from Pennsylvania; Federalist

Wynkoop, who was of Dutch ancestry, owned a large farm called Vredensburg and was reputed to make the finest cider, which he sold in Philadelphia. He was elected at age twenty-three to the Pennsylvania provincial assembly. He served as a major in Bucks County Associated Battalions and was a member of the general committee of safety during the war. Wynkoop suffered a personal tragedy during the Revolution when Hessians broke into his home late at night and so frightened his wife that she ran outside and fell into an open well. He was a member of the Continental Congress and the Confederation Congress and, at the age of fifty-two, was elected to the First Federal Congress. He served as an associate justice for Bucks County until his death in 1816. Wynkoop was very tall, at least six feet four inches, and Alexander Hamilton quipped that everyone had to look up to Mr. Wynkoop.

Acknowledgments

This is a book about how and why the Bill of Rights came into existence. It is neither a legal treatise on the first ten amendments nor a biography of James Madison. Other scholars have provided learned and often brilliant books and articles on both topics. Their work helped make mine possible. But two indispensable collections deserve my deepest gratitude. I want to extend my thanks to Charlene Bangs Bickford, Kenneth R. Bowling, Linda Grant DePauw, and Helen E. Veit, the scholars who produced the multivolume *Documentary History of the First Federal Congress* and the more compact *Creating the Bill of Rights: The Documentary Record from the First Federal Congress.* This gathering of primary sources has provided scholars with the wealth of materials needed to explore the politics of the early republic. My thanks as well to Merrill Jensen, John Kaminski, Gaspare J. Saladino, Richard Leffler, and Charles H. Schoenleber, whose *Documentary History of the Ratification of the Constitution* has given us access to the riches of the archives on this subject. And my appreciation extends to the historians who labored, and still labor, on publication of the papers of leading figures of the Revolutionary generation and to the many scholars whose books and articles appear in my bibliography.

As this project progressed, it was aided by the astute criticism of colleagues and friends. Angelo Angelis, Meg Berlin, Stuart Blumin, Cecelia

Hartsell, Cindy Lobel, and Philip Papas added their wisdom and gave their advice at critical moments in the writing of this book. They should be credited with many of its best features and blamed for none of its failures.

Two remarkable young historians helped me from the inception of this project to its completion. Sarah Pearlman Shapiro, whose research skills are matched only by her good humor, located many of the most obscure sources needed and brought order to the chaos of my footnotes. My former student Michael Hattem, who is a walking bibliography on the eighteenth century, found time to answer a number of SOS e-mails despite his busy schedule as a PhD student at Yale and the author of an important history blog.

This is the fifth book that my agent Dan Green has played a critical role in bringing to fruition. He not only finds a home for my projects but also reads every word as it comes off the computer. He never ceases to amaze me with the depth of his historical knowledge and his ability to make suggestions that improve the manuscript without deflating the ego of its author. And at every step of the way, my editor Thomas LeBien has demonstrated why he is so respected by historians of American history. His suggestions, both substantive and stylistic, improved this book's content and its presentation.

Over the many years that I have labored in the eighteenth century, my children, Hannah and Matthew, have been my anchor to the here and now. This has never been more true than during the writing of this book. While I was following James Madison's efforts to create a Bill of Rights, both of my children got married and my first grandchild was born—events I feel certain would make even the grumpy Elbridge Gerry smile. It is a joy to dedicate this book to my granddaughter, Talulla Thomas Joyce.

Carol Berkin
New York City, 2014

Bibliography

Primary Sources

———

Abbot, W. W., ed. *The Papers of George Washington, Confederation Series,* Vol. 6. University Press of Virginia, 1997.

Annals of the Congress of the United States, 42 vols. Gales and Seaton, 1834–1856.

Ballagh, James Curtis, ed. *The Letters of Richard Henry Lee,* Vol. 2, *1779–1794.* Macmillan, 1914.

Boyd, Julian P., ed. *The Papers of Thomas Jefferson,* Vol. 12. Princeton University Press, 1955.

Butler, Pierce. *The Letters of Pierce Butler, 1790–1794: Nation Building and Enterprise in the New American Republic.* University of South Carolina Press, 2007.

Cogan, Neil H., ed. *The Complete Bill of Rights: The Drafts, Debates, Sources, and Origins.* Oxford University Press, 1997.

Documentary History of the First Federal Congress, 1789–1791 (DHFFC), Vols. III, X, XI, XV, XVI, XVII. Johns Hopkins University Press, 1872–2004.

Elliot, Jonathan, ed. *The Debates in Several States on the Adoption of the Federal Constitution.* Published under the sanction of congress, Library of Congress, 1845.

Farrand, Max. *The Records of the Federal Convention of 1787,* Vol. 2. Yale University Press, 1967.

The Federalist Papers. Tribeca, 2001.

Gales, Joseph. *The Debates and Proceedings in the Congress of the United States: With an Appendix, Containing Important State Papers and Public Documents,* Vol. 2. Gales and Seaton, 1834.

Henry, J. Winfield, ed. *Letters and Papers of Governor John Henry of Maryland.* George W. King Printing Company, 1904.

The Huntington Letters: In the Possession of Julia Chester Wells. Appleton Press, 1897.

Jensen, Merrill, John P. Kaminski, Gaspare J. Saladino, Richard Leffler, and Charles H. Schoenleber, eds. *The Documentary History of the Ratification of the Constitution,* 26 vols. State Historical Society of Wisconsin, 1976.

Maclay, William. *Journal of William Maclay, United States Senator from Pennsylvania.* Forgotten Books, 2012.

"Notes of Major William Pierce on the Federal Convention of 1787," *American Historical Review,* Vol. 3, No. 2 (January 1898).

Rakove, Jack N., ed. *James Madison: Writings.* Library of America, 1999.

Records of the United States Congress. National Archives.

Rutland, Edward A., ed. *The Papers of George Mason*, Vol. 3. University of North Carolina Press, 1970.

Rutland, Robert A., Charles F. Hobson, William M. E. Rachal, and Frederika J. Teute, eds. *The Papers of James Madison*, Vol. 10, *27 May 1787–3 March 1788*; and Vol. 12. University of Chicago Press, 1977.

Syrett, Harold C., ed. *The Papers of Alexander Hamilton,* 26 vols. Columbia University Press, 1961.

Veit, Helen E., Kenneth R. Bowling, and Charlene Bangs, Bickford, eds. *Creating the Bill of Rights: The Documentary Record from the First Federal Congress.* Johns Hopkins University Press, 1991.

Secondary Sources

————

Books

Amar, Akhil Reed. *The Bill of Rights: Creation and Reconstruction.* Yale University Press, 2000.

Bailyn, Bernard. *The Ideological Origins of the American Revolution.* Belknap Press of Harvard University Press, 1992.

————. *The Ordeal of Thomas Hutchinson.* Belknap Press of Harvard University Press, 1974.

Banning, Lance. *The Sacred Fire of Liberty: James Madison and the Founding of the Federal Republic.* Cornell University Press, 1998.

Beeman, Richard. *Plain, Honest Men: The Making of the American Constitution.* Random House, reprint, 2010.

Berkin, Carol. *A Brilliant Solution: Inventing the American Constitution.* Harcourt, 2002.

Bernstein, Richard B. *Are We to Be a Nation?* Harvard University Press, 1987.

Bodenhammer, David J. *The Revolutionary Constitution.* Oxford University Press, 2012.

Boudinot, Elias. *The Age of Revelation, or, The Age of Reason Shewn to Be an Age of Infidelity.* Asbury Dickins, 1801.

Brant, Irving. *The Bill of Rights: Its Origins and Meaning.* Bobbs-Merrill, 1965.

Broadwater, Jeff. *George Mason, Forgotten Founder.* University of North Carolina Press, 2006.

Brookhiser, Richard. *Alexander Hamilton, American.* Simon & Schuster, 2000.

———. *James Madison.* Basic Books, 2011.

Burrows, Edwin G., and Michael Wallace. *Gotham: A History of New York City to 1898.* Oxford University Press, 2000.

Caldwell, John. *Thomas Scott: Western Federalist.* Five Rhinos, 2008.

Conley, Patrick T., and John P. Kaminsky. *The Bill of Rights and the States: The Colonial and Revolutionary Origins of American Liberties.* Madison House, 1992.

Cornell, Saul. *The Other Founders: Anti-Federalism and the Dissenting Tradition in America, 1788–1828.* University of North Carolina Press, 1999.

Deas, Anne Izard, ed. *Correspondence of Mr. Ralph Izard of South Carolina from the Year 1774 to 1804 with a Short Memoir,* Vol. 1, C. S. Francis, 1844.

De Rose, Chris. *Founding Rivals: Madison vs. Monroe, the Bill of Rights, and the Election That Saved the Nation.* Regnery History, 2013.

Dougherty, Kevin. *Collective Action Under the Articles of Confederation.* Cambridge University Press, 2000.

Folsom, George. *History of Saco and Biddeford: With Notices of Other Early Settlements, and of Proprietary Governments, in Maine, Including the Provinces of New Somersetshire and Lygonia.* A. C. Putnam, 1830.

Freeman, Joanne. *Affairs of Honor: National Politics in the New Republic.* Yale University Press, 2002.

Gillespie, Michael Allen, and Michael Lienesch. *Ratifying the Constitution.* University Press of Kansas, 1992.

Gross, Robert A. *The Minutemen and Their World.* Hill and Wang, 2001.

Gutzman, Kevin. *James Madison and the Making of America.* St. Martin's, 2012.

Heideking, Jurgen. *The Constitution Before the Judgment Seat: The Prehistory and Ratification of the American Constitution, 1787–1791,* ed. John P. Kaminski and Richard Leffler. University of Virginia Press, 2012.

Hoffer, Peter C. *Cry Liberty: The Great Stono River Slave Rebellion of 1739.* Oxford University Press, 2011.

Hoffman, Ronald, and Peter J. Albert, eds. *The Bill of Rights: Government Proscribed.* University of Virginia Press, 1998.

Hunemorder, Markus. *The Society of the Cincinnati: Conspiracy and Distrust in Early America.* Berghahn, 2006.

Jensen, Merrill. *The Articles of Confederation: An Interpretation of the Social-Constitutional History of the American Revolution, 1774–1781.* University of Wisconsin Press, 1959.

Kammen, Michael. *A Machine That Would Go of Itself: The Constitution in American Culture.* Vintage, 1987.

Kars, Marjoleine. *Breaking Loose Together: The Regulator Rebellion in Pre-Revolutionary North Carolina.* University of North Carolina Press, 2001.

Kenny, Kevin. *Peaceable Kingdom Lost: The Paxton Boys and the Destruction of William Penn's Holy Experiment.* Oxford University Press, 2011.

Ketcham, Ralph. *James Madison: A Biography.* University of Virginia Press, 1990.

———, ed. *The Anti-Federalist Papers and the Constitutional Convention Debates.* Signet Classics, 2003.

Klein, Milton M. *The Empire State: A History of New York.* Cornell University Press, 2005.

Labunski, Richard. *James Madison and the Struggle for the Bill of Rights.* Oxford University Press, 2006.

Lee, John K. *George Clinton: Master Builder of the Empire State.* Syracuse University Press, 2009.

Lepore, Jill. *New York Burning: Liberty, Slavery, and Conspiracy in Eighteenth-Century Manhattan.* Vintage, reprint ed., 2006.

Levy, Leonard W. *Origins of the Bill of Rights.* Yale University Press, 1999.

Maier, Pauline. *American Scripture: Making the Declaration of Independence.* Vintage, 1998.

———. *Ratification: The People Debate the Constitution, 1787–1788.* Simon & Schuster, 2011.

Main, Jackson Turner. *The Antifederalists: Critics of the Constitution, 1781–1788.* University of North Carolina Press, 1961.

Marshall, James V. *The United States Manual of Biography and History.* James B. Smith and Company, 1856.

McClanahan, Brion. *The Founding Fathers Guide to the Constitution.* Regnery, 2012.

McDonald, Forrest. *States' Rights and the Union: Imperium in Imperio, 1776–1876.* University Press of Kansas, reprint ed., 2002.

McMaster, John Bach, and Frederick Stone. *Pennsylvania and the Federal Constitution, 1787–1788.* Liberty Fund, 2013.

Meleney, John C. *The Public Life of Aedanus Burke: Revolutionary Republican in Post-Revolutionary South Carolina.* University of South Carolina Press, 1989.

Merrill, George Drew. *History of Coos County, New Hampshire.* W. A. Fergusson and Company, 1888.

Middlekauf, Robert S. *The Glorious Cause*. Oxford University Press, 1982.

Morgan, Edmund S. *American Slavery, American Freedom*. Norton, 2003.

———. *The Birth of the Republic, 1763–89*, 4th ed. University of Chicago Press, 2013.

Perdue, Theda, ed. *Cherokee Editor: The Writings of Elias Boudinot*. University of Georgia Press, 1996.

Ragosta, John A. *Wellspring of Liberty: How Virginia's Religious Dissenters Helped Win the American Revolution and Secure Religious Liberty*. Oxford University Press, 2010.

Rakove, Jack N., ed. *The Annotated U.S. Constitution and Declaration of Independence*. Harvard University Press, 2009.

Rice, James D. *Tales from a Revolution: Bacon's Rebellion and the Transformation of Early America*. Oxford University Press, 2013.

Rutland, Robert A. *The Birth of the Bill of Rights, 1776–1791*. University of North Carolina Press, 1955.

———. *James Madison: The Founding Father*. University of Missouri Press, 1997.

Schechter, Stephen L., and Richard B. Bernstein, eds. *Contexts of the Bill of Rights*. New York State Commission on the Bicentennial of the U.S. Constitution, 1990.

Schwartz, Bernard. *The Roots of the Bill of Rights*, Vol. 3. Chelsea House, 1971.

Stewart, David O. *The Summer of 1787: The Men Who Invented the Constitution*. Simon & Schuster, America Collection, 2008.

Storing, Herbert J. *What the Antifederalists Were For: The Political Thought of the Opponents of the Constitution*. University of Chicago Press, 1981.

Sumner, William Graham. *Robert Morris*. Dodd, Mead, 1892.

Swift, Jonathan. *A Tale of a Tub*. George Routledge and Sons, 1889.

Szatmary, David P. *Shays' Rebellion: The Making of an Agrarian Insurrection*. University of Massachusetts Press, 1984.

Tracy, Cyrus Mason. *Standard History of Essex County, Massachusetts, Embracing a History of the County from Its First Settlement to the Present Time: With a History and Description of Its Towns and Cities*. C. F. Jewett and Company, 1878.

Troxler, Carole W. *Farming Dissenters: The Regulator Movement in Piedmont North Carolina*. North Carolina Office of Archives and History, 2011.

Washburn, Wilcomb E. *The Governor and the Rebel: A History of Bacon's Rebellion in Virginia*. Norton 1972.

Waters, John J., Jr. *The Otis Family in Provincial and Revolutionary Massachusetts*. University of North Carolina Press, 1968.

Watkins, William. *Reclaiming the American Revolution: The Kentucky and Virginia Resolutions and Their Legacy*. Palgrave Macmillan, 2008.

Weiner, Greg. *Madison's Metronome: The Constitution, Majority Rule, and the Tempo of American Politics.* University of Kansas Press, 2012.

Widmer, Edward. *American Speeches: Political Oratory from the Revolution to the Civil War.* Library of America, 2006.

Wilder, Craig Steven. *In the Company of Black Men: The African Influence on African American Culture in New York City.* New York University Press, 2001.

Wood, Gordon S. *The American Revolution.* Modern Library, 2002.

———. *Empire of Liberty: A History of the Early Republic,* 1789–1815. Oxford University Press, 2011.

———. *The Radicalism of the American Revolution.* Vintage, 1993.

Articles

Aldrich, John H., and Ruth Grant. "The Antifederalists, the First Congress, and the First Parties," *Journal of Politics,* Vol. 55, No. 2 (May 1993), 205–326.

Altman, John A. "The Articles and the Constitution: Similar in Nature, Different in Design," *Pennsylvania Legacies,* Vol. 3, No. 1 (May 2003), 20–21.

Amar, Akhil Reed. "The Bill of Rights as a Constitution," *Yale Law Journal,* Vol. 100, No. 5 (1991), 1131–1210.

Bowling, Kenneth R. "Overshadowed by States' Rights: Ratification of the Federal Bill of Rights," in Ronald Hoffman and Peter J. Albert, eds., *The Bill of Rights: Government Proscribed.* University Press of Virginia, 1997.

———. " 'A Tub to the Whale': The Founding Fathers and Adoption of the Federal Bill of Rights," *Journal of the Early Republic,* Vol. 8, (Autumn 1988), 223–51.

Bristow, Weston. "William Grayson: A Study in Virginia Biography of the Eighteenth Century," *Richmond College Historical Papers* (June 1917), 74–117.

Cheves, Langdon. "Izard of South Carolina," *South Carolina Historical and Genealogical Magazine.* Walkers, Evans, and Cogswell Company, 1900. Vol. 2, 208.

Christman, Margaret C. S. "Unraveling a Mistaken Identity Profile," *Smithsonian National Portrait Gallery News,* Vol. 1, No. 3 (Fall 2000), 10.

Coghlan, Francis. "Pierce Butler, 1744–1822, First Senator from South Carolina," *South Carolina Historical Magazine,* Vol. 78, No. 2 (April 1977), 104–19.

Cornell, Saul. "The Changing Fortunes of the Anti-Federalists," *Northwestern University Law Review,* Vol. 84, No. 1 (1989), 41–45.

———. "Moving Beyond the Canon of Traditional Constitutional History: Antifederalists, the Bill of Rights, and the Promise of Post-Modern Historiography," *Law and History Review,* Vol. 84, No. 1 (1989), 39–74.

Crowl, Philip A. "Anti-Federalism in Maryland, 1787–1788," *William and Mary Quarterly,* 3rd Series, Vol. 4, No. 4 (October 1947), 446–69.

Dowdy, Diana Dru. " 'A School for Stoicism': Thomas Tudor Tucker and the Republican Age," *South Carolina Historical Magazine,* Vol. 96, No. 2 (April 1995), 102–18.

Duncan, Christopher M. "Men of a Different Faith: The Antifederalist Ideal in Early American Political Thought," *Polity,* Vol. 26, No. 3 (Spring 1994), 387–415.

Finkelman, Paul. "James Madison and the Bill of Rights: A Reluctant Paternity," *Supreme Court Review* (1990), 301–47.

Gerber, Scott D. "Roger Sherman and the Bill of Rights," *Polity,* Vol. 28, No. 4 (Summer 1996), 521–40.

Gibson, Alan. "Veneration and Vigilance: James Madison and Public Opinion, 1785–1800," *Review of Politics,* Vol. 67, No. 1 (2005), 5–35.

Hull, Richard W. "John Hathorn, Warwick's Forgotten Patriot," *Warwick Valley Dispatch* (August 4, 2014).

Hutson, James H. "The Birth of the Bill of Rights: The State of Current Scholarship," *Prologue,* Vol. 20, No. 3 (September 1988), 143–61.

———. "A Nauseous Project," *Wilson Quarterly,* Vol. 15, No. 1 (Winter 1991), 56–70.

Hylton, J. Gordon. "Virginia and the Ratification of the Bill of Rights, 1789–1791," *University of Richmond Law Review,* Vol. 25, (1991).

Kaminski, John. "The Making of the Bill of Rights 1787–1792," in Stephen L. Schechter and Richard B. Bernstein, eds., *Contexts of the Bill of Rights.* New York State Commission on the Bicentennial of the United States Constitution, 1990.

Kenyon, Cecelia M. "Men of Little Faith: The Antifederalists on the Nature of Representative Government," *William and Mary Quarterly,* 3rd Series. Vol. 12, No. 1 (1955), 3–43.

Kukla, Jon. "A Spectrum of Sentiments: Virginia's Federalists, Antifederalists, and 'Federalists Who Are for Amendments,' 1787–1788," *Virginia Magazine of History and Biography,* Vol. 96, No. 3 (July 1988), 276–96.

Lamplugh, George R. "The Importance of Being Truculent: James Gunn, the Chatham Militia, and Georgia Politics, 1782–1789," *Georgia Historical Quarterly,* Vol. 80, No. 2 (Summer 1996), 227–45.

———. " 'Oh the Colossus! The Colossus!' James Jackson and the Jeffersonian Republican Party in Georgia, 1796–1806," *Journal of the Early Republic,* Vol. 9, No. 3 (Autumn 1989), 315–34.

Leibiger, Stuart. "James Madison and Amendments to the Constitution, 1787–1789: 'Parchment Barriers,'" *Journal of Southern History,* Vol. 59, No. 3 (1993), 441–68.

Lutz, Donald S. "The State Constitutional Pedigree of the U.S. Bill of Rights," *Publius,* Vol. 22, No. 2 (1992), 19–45.

Matson, Cathy. "Liberty, Jealousy, and Union: The New York Economy in the 1780s," in *New York in the Age of the Constitution, 1775–1800*, ed. Paul A. Gilje and William Pencak. Fairleigh Dickinson University Press, 1992.

Matthews, Albert, ed. "Journal of William Loughton Smith, 1790–1791," *Proceedings of the Massachusetts Historical Society* (October 1917).

Nedelsky, Jennifer. "Confining Democratic Politics: Antifederalists, Federalists, and the Constitution," *Harvard Law Review*, Vol. 96, No. 1 (1982).

Nelson, William E. "Reason and Compromise in the Establishment of the Federal Constitution, 1787–1801," *William and Mary Quarterly*, 3rd Series, Vol. 44, No. 3 (July 1987), 458–84.

Proctor, A. Douglas. "Colonel Jeremiah Wadsworth," *Connecticut Society of the Sons of the American Revolution Newsletter*, 1990.

Rakove, Jack N. "James Madison and the Bill of Rights: A Broader Context," *Presidential Studies Quarterly*, Vol. 22, No. 4 (1992), 667–77.

———. "The Structure of Politics at the Accession of George Washington," in Richard Beeman, Stephen Botein and Edward C. Carter, eds., *Beyond Confederation: Origins of the Constitution and American National Identity*. University of North Carolina Press, 1987, 261–94.

Rosenblatt, Betsy L. "New York State's Role in the Creation and Adoption of the Bill of Rights," *New York History*, Vol. 72, No. 4 (October 1991), 407–20.

Stone, Eben F. "A Sketch of Tristram Dalton," *Historical Collections of the Essex Institute*, Vol. 25, Nos. 1, 2, 3, (January, February, March 1888), 1–29.

Weber, Paul J. "Madison's Opposition to a Second Convention," *Polity*, Vol. 20, No. 3 (Spring 1988), 498–517.

Wood, Gordon S. "Interests and Disinterestedness in the Making of the Constitution," in Richard Beeman, Stephen Botein and Edward C. Carter, eds., *Beyond Confederation: Origins of the Constitution and American National Identity*. University of North Carolina Press, 1987, 69–112.

Wynkoop, Henry, and Joseph M. Beatty Jr. "The Letters of Judge Henry Wynkoop, Representative from Pennsylvania to the First Congress of the United States," *Pennsylvania Magazine of History and Biography*, Vol. 38, No. 1 (1914), 39–64.

Notes

Chapter One

1. For a full account of the constitutional convention, see Carol Berkin, *A Brilliant Solution: Inventing the American Constitution* (Harcourt, 2003); see also David O. Stewart, *The Summer of 1787: The Men Who Invented the Constitution* (Simon & Schuster, America Collection, 2008); Richard Beeman, *Plain, Honest Men: The Making of the American Constitution* (Random House, 2010); Richard B. Bernstein, *Are We to Be a Nation?* (Harvard University Press, 1987).

2. On the Articles of Confederation, see Merrill Jensen, *The Articles of Confederation: An Interpretation of the Social-Constitutional History of the American Revolution, 1774–1781* (University of Wisconsin Press, 1959); see also Kevin Dougherty, *Collective Action Under the Articles of Confederation* (Cambridge University Press, 2000), and John A. Altman, "The Articles and the Constitution: Similar in Nature, Different in Design," *Pennsylvania Legacies,* Vol. 3, No. 1 (May 2003), 20–21.

3. For a discussion of the problems facing the Confederation government, see Berkin, *Brilliant Solution,* chap. 1.

4. "Notes of Major William Pierce on the Federal Convention of 1787," *American Historical Review,* Vol. 3, No. 2 (January 1898), 314.

5. Max Farrand, *The Records of the Federal Convention of 1787* (Yale University Press, 1911), Vol. 2, 582–89; For more on Sherman's view on a bill of rights as unnecessary, see Scott D. Gerber, "Roger Sherman and the Bill of Rights," *Polity,* Vol. 28, No. 4 (Summer 1996), 521–40.

Chapter Two

1. On the ideology of the American Revolution, see Bernard Bailyn, *The Ideological Origins of the American Revolution* (Belknap Press of Harvard University Press, 1992); see also Gordon S. Wood, *The Radicalism of the American Revolution* (Vintage, 1993).

2. For a collection of the arguments made by opponents of the Constitution, see Herbert Storing, *What the Antifederalists Were For: The Political Thought of the Opponents of the Constitution* (University of Chicago Press, 1981); Cecelia M. Kenyon, "Men of Little Faith: The Antifederalists on the Nature of Representative Government," *William and Mary Quarterly*, 3rd Series, Vol. 12, No. 1 (1955), 3–43; Christopher M. Duncan, "Men of a Different Faith: The Antifederalist Ideal in Early American Political Thought," *Polity*, Vol. 26, No. 3 (Spring 1994), 387–415; Saul Cornell, *The Other Founders* (University of North Carolina Press, 1999).

3. For biographies of James Madison, see for example, Ralph Ketcham, *James Madison* (University of Virginia Press, 1990); Richard Brookhiser, *James Madison* (Basic Books, 2011); Kevin Gutzman, *James Madison and the Making of America* (St. Martin's, 2012). For Ames's description, see Gordon S. Wood, *Empire of Liberty: A History of the Early Republic, 1789–1815* (Oxford University Press, 2011). For William Pierce's description, see "Notes of Major William Pierce on the Federal Convention of 1787," *American Historical Review*, Vol. 3, No. 2 (January 1898), 310–34, 331.

4. For Madison's concern about opposition to the Constitution in the Confederation Congress, see James Madison to George Washington, September 30, 1787, *The Papers of James Madison*, Vol. 10, *27 May 1787–3 March 1788*, ed. Robert A. Rutland, Charles F. Hobson, William M. E. Rachal, and Frederika J. Teute. (University of Chicago Press, 1977), 179–81. For Richard Henry Lee's actions in the Confederation Congress, see Richard Henry Lee to George Mason, October 1, 1787, Mason Papers, Vol. 3, 996–97, LC.

5. Quoted in Paul Finkelman, "James Madison and the Bill of Rights: A Reluctant Paternity," *Supreme Court Review* (1990), 301–47, 320.

6. For a biography of George Clinton, see John K. Lee, *George Clinton: Master Builder of the Empire State* (Syracuse University Press, 2009). See also Milton M. Klein, *The Empire State: A History of New York* (Cornell University Press, 2005); Cathy Matson, "Liberty, Jealousy, and Union: The New York Economy in the 1780s," in *New York in the Age of the Constitution, 1775–1800*, ed. Paul A.

Gilje and William Pencak (Fairleigh Dickinson University Press, 1992), 112–50; Edwin G. Burrows and Michael Wallace, *Gotham: A History of New York City to 1898* (Oxford University Press, 2000), 279–81.

7. See Virginia Ratifying Convention debates, June 7, 1788, in Jonathan Elliot, *The Debates in Several State Conventions on the Adoption of the Federal Constitution* (J. B. Lippincott, 1901), Vol. 3, 104.

8. See Storing, *What the Antifederalists Were For,* 7–8.

9. Thomas Jefferson to John Adams, August 30, 1787, in Julian Boyd, ed., *The Papers of Thomas Jefferson,* Vol. 12 (Princeton University Press, 1955), 66–69.

10. *The Federal Farmer,* Vol. 7, quoted in Storing, *What the Antifederalists Were For,* 17.

Chapter Three

1. For George Mason's objections, see *Virginia Journal,* November 22, 1787; see also *Merrill Jensen,* John P. Kaminski, Gaspare J. Saladino, Richard Leffler, and Charles H. Schoenleber, eds., *The Documentary History of the Ratification of the Constitution* (State Historical Society of Wisconsin, 1976), Vol. 8, 174–75. For a biography of Mason, see Jeff Broadwater, *George Mason, Forgotten Founder* (University of North Carolina Press, 2006). For Richard Henry Lee's critique, see James Curtis Ballagh, ed., *The Letters of Richard Henry Lee,* Vol. 2, *1779–1794* (Macmillan, 1914), 442–44. James Wilson's argument against the necessity of a bill of rights was published in *The Pennsylvania Packet,* October 10, 1787. For a discussion of the speech, see John Bach McMaster and Frederick Stone, *Pennsylvania and the Federal Constitution, 1787–1788* (Liberty Fund, 2013), chap. 1.

2. Alexander Hamilton, James Madison, and John Jay, *The Federalist Papers* (Tribeca, 2001); see also George W. Carey and James McClellan, eds., *The Federalists* (Liberty Fund, 2001), 546–56.

3. On the ratification conventions, see Pauline Maier, *Ratification: The People Debate the Constitution, 1787–1788* (Simon & Schuster, 2011). See also Jensen et al., *Documentary History;* Jonathan Elliot, ed., *The Debates in the Several State Conventions on the Adoption of the Federal Constitution,* 5 vols. (Published Under the Sanction of Congress, Library of Congress, 1845); Michael Allen Gillespie and Michael Lienesch, *Ratifying the Constitution* (University Press of Kansas, 1992).

4. *Philadelphia Independent Gazetteer,* April 4, 1788, in Jensen, et al., *Documentary*

History Vol. 9, 614. See also Richard Labunski, *James Madison and the Struggle for the Bill of Rights* (Oxford University Press, 2006), 27.

5. Elliot, *Debates,* Vol. 3, 652.

6. Ibid., Vol. 2, 401; see also Betsy L. Rosenblatt, "New York State's Role in the Creation and Adoption of the Bill of Rights," *New York History,* Vol. 72, No. 4 (October 1991), 407–20.

7. For a discussion of the opposition at the Philadelphia convention to a second convention, see Paul J. Weber, "Madison's Opposition to a Second Convention," *Polity,* Vol. 20, No. 3 (Spring 1988), 498–517; Pinckney's comment is on 506. See also Max Farrand, *The Records of the Federal Convention of 1787* (Yale University Press, 1911), Vol. 2, 632.

Chapter Four

1. James Madison to George *Lee Turberville, November 2, 1788, in Robert A. Rutland, Charles F. Hobson, eds.,* The Papers of James Madison (University Press of Virginia, 1977), Vol. 11, 330–32.

2. James Madison to Edmund Randolph, November 2, 1788, ibid., 328–30; James Madison to Thomas Jefferson, August 23, 1788, in Julian P. Boyd, ed., *The Papers of Thomas Jefferson* (Princeton University Press, 1956), Vol. 13, 539–41.

3. W. W. Abbot, ed., *The Papers of George Washington, Confederation Series* (University Press of Virginia, 1997), Vol. 6: George Washington to James McHenry, July 31, 1788, 409–10; George Washington to Benjamin Lincoln, August 28, 1788, 482–83; George Washington to Charles Pettit, August 16, 1788, 447–49.

4. For the text of the New York Ratifying Convention Circular Letter to the Governors of the Several States, July 26, 1788, see Harold C. Syrett, ed., *The Papers of Alexander Hamilton* (Columbia University Press 1961), Vol. 5, 196. For a discussion of efforts to call a second convention and the Federalists' anxiety over the possibility, see Jurgen Heideking, *The Constitution Before the Judgment Seat: The Prehistory and Ratification of the American Constitution, 1787–1791,* ed. John Kaminski and Richard Leffler, (University of Virginia Press, 2012). On the difficulties a second convention would entail, see Richard Labunski, *James Madison and the Struggle for the Bill of Rights* (Oxford University Press, 2006), 52–55.

5. Rutland et al., *Papers of James Madison,* Vol. 11: James Madison to Alexander

Hamilton, June 27, 1788, 181–82; and James Madison to George Washington, June 27, 1788, 182–83.

6. For Madison's campaign for election to the Congress, see Chris De Rose, *Founding Rivals: Madison vs. Monroe, the Bill of Rights, and the Election That Saved the Nation* (Regnery History, 2013). See also Labunski, *James Madison,* 130–75; Kenneth R. Bowling, " 'A Tub to the Whale,' " *Journal of the Early Republic,* Vol. 8, No. 3 (Autumn 1988), 231–33.

7. Edward Carrington to James Madison, November 15, 1788, in Rutland et al., *Papers of James Madison,* Vol. 11, 345–46.

8. Ibid.: James Madison to Edmund Randolph, November 23, 1788, 362–64; and James Madison to George Washington, December 2, 1788, 376–78.

9. Ibid.: George Lee Turberville to James Madison, November 16, 1788, 346–47.

10. Ibid.: James Madison to George Eve, January 2, 1789, 404–6.

11. Ibid.: James Madison to Thomas Jefferson, October 17, 1788, 295–300.

12. Ibid.: James Madison to George Eve, January 2, 1789, 404–6.

13. See Heideking, *Constitution Before the Judgment Seat,* 400.

14. Alexander J. Dallas's Notes of the Pennsylvania Ratification Convention, November 28, 1787, in Merrill Jensen, John P. Kaminski, Gaspare J. Saladino, Richard Leffler, and Charles H. Schoenleber, eds., *The Documentary History of the Ratification of the Constitution* (State Historical Society of Wisconsin, 1988–1993), Vol. 2, 383–87.

15. Letters of Agrippa, 16, *Massachusetts Gazette,* November 1787–February 1788, ibid., 863–68; James Madison to Thomas Jefferson, October 17, 1788, in Rutland et al., *Papers of James Madison,* Vol. 11, 295–300.

16. James Madison to Thomas Jefferson, October 17, 1788, ibid.

Chapter Five

1. *Documentary History of the First Federal Congress,* 1789–1791 (DHFFC), Vols. III, X, XI, XV, XVI, XVII, (Johns Hopkins University Press, 1872–2004), XV, 71.

2. Ibid.: 15–16.

3. Ibid.: Fisher Ames to John Lowell, March 4, 1789, 9.

4. Ibid.: Ann Gerry to Samuel R. Gerry, March 8, 1789, 43; for a discussion of travel difficulties, 19–22.

5. Ibid.: "Letter from a Member of Congress," 58.

6. Ibid.: Comte de Moustier to Comte de Montmorin, March 20, 1789, 84; "Letter from New York," 154.

7. Ibid.: William Maclay to Benjamin Rush, March 19, 1789, 78; Fisher Ames to George R. Minot, March 25, 1789, 126.

8. Ibid.: Richard Bassett to George Read, March 21–22, 1789, 90–91; Richard Bassett to George Read, March 29, 1789, 145.

9. For a list of congressional members' residences in New York, see DHFFC, XVII, 1739–42; for a discussion of how congressmen lived in New York, see DHFFC, XV, xxii-xxv.

10. William Maclay to Tench Coxe, March 30, 1789, DHFFC, XV, 159–60.

11. Ibid.: James Madison to Thomas Jefferson, March 29, 1789, 147–49.

12. Ibid.: Fisher Ames to George R. Minot, April 4, 1789, 196.

13. Elbridge Gerry to James Warren, March 22, 1789, ibid., 91–93; William Ellery to Benjamin Huntington, September 8, 1789, DHFFC, XVII, 1489–90.

14. See Elias Boudinot, *The Age of Revelation, or, The Age of Reason Shewn to Be an Age of Infidelity* (Asbury Dickins, 1801); for the writings of Elias Boudinot's namesake, see Theda Perdue, ed., *Cherokee Editor: The Writings of Elias Boudinot* (University of Georgia Press, 1996).

15. Fisher Ames to George R. Minot, May 3, 1789, DHFFC, XV, 436–38; George Beckwith, "Conversations with Different People," undated, 1789, DHFFC, XVII, 1727.

16. Fisher Ames to George R. Minot, April 4, 1789, DHFFC, XV, 196. See my back matter for biographical sketches of members of Congress.

17. John Quincy Adams to James Bridge, September 21, 1789, DHFFC, XVII, 1595.

18. For a full discussion of the newspaper coverage of the House's first session, see Introductory Essay, DHFFC, X, xi–xxviii.

19. Peter Muhlenberg to Benjamin Rush, March 18, 1789, DHFFC, XV, 75–76; "Letter from New York," *Massachusetts Centinel,* April 11, 1789, in DHFFC, XV, 212.

20. Ibid.: Elias Boudinot to Hannah Boudinot, April 24, 1789, 334; Elias Boudinot to William Bradford Jr., April 24, 1789, 340; Theodorick Bland to St. George Tucker, April 15, 1789, 265.

21. George Washington's First Inaugural Address, April 30, 1789, *Records of the United States Congress,* National Archives.

22. Patrick Henry to William Grayson, March 31, 1789, DHFFC, XV, 166–68.

23. Ibid.: Ralph Izard to Thomas Jefferson, April 3, 1789, 190–91; Fisher Ames to William Tudor, April 1, 1789, 180. For Izard to Jefferson, see also Helen F. Veit, Kenneth R. Bowling, and Charlene Bands Bickford, eds., *Creating the Bill of Rights: The Documentary Record from the First Federal Congress* (Johns Hopkins University Press, 1991), 227. (Hereafter cited as Veit.)

24. Edmund Randolph to James Madison, March 27, 1789, DHFFC, XV, 138–39, and Veit, 223–24; Ezra Stiles to William Samuel Johnson, April 3, 1789, DHFFC, XV, 192–93, and Veit, 227–28; Ezra Ripley to George Thatcher, March 30, 1789, DHFFC, XV, 160–61.

25. James Madison to Samuel Johnston, June 21, 1789, DHFFC, XVI, 827–28.

26. James Madison to Edmund Pendleton, April 8, 1789, DHFFC, XV, 225.

Chapter Six

1. For the Virginia petition, see DHFFC, III, 47–48; for the debate on the petition, see DHFFC, X, 430–32; 444–46.

2. For the New York petition, see DHFFC, III, 50; DHFFC, X, 472.

3. James Madison to Thomas Jefferson, March 29, 1789, DHFFC, XV, 147–49.

4. DHFFC, X, 780.

5. DHFFC, XI, 803, 804, 805, and for the full debate as reported in various newspapers, 803–36.

6. For Madison's notes for this debate on June 10, see DHFFC, XVI, 723–25.

7. DHFFC, XI, 822–23.

8. For Madison's proposed amendments, see my Appendix; see also Jack N. Rakove, ed., *James Madison: Writings* (Library of America, 1999), 437–52.

9. For Jackson's remarks, see DHFFC, XI 827–30, and Veit, 86–89.

10. For Gerry's remarks, see DHFFC, XI, 830–35.

Chapter Seven

1. Fisher Ames to Thomas Dwight, June 11, 1789, DHFFC, XVI, 748–49, and Veit, 247; Fisher Ames to George R. Minot, June 12, 1789, DHFFC, XVI, 755–56, and Veit, 247–48; George Clymer to Tench Coxe, June 28, 1789, in DHFFC, XVI, 874, and Veit, 255.

2. Abraham Baldwin to Joel Barlow, June 14, 1789, DHFFC, XVI, 774–75, and Veit, 250; Thomas Fitzsimons to Benjamin Rush, June 15, 1789, DHFFC, XVI, 782, and Veit, 250.

3. William Grayson to Patrick Henry, June 12, 1789, DHFFC, XVI, 759, and Veit, 248–49.

4. George Lee Turberville to James Madison, June 16, 1789, DHFFC, XVI, 791–93, and Veit, 251–52.

5. Joseph Jones to James Madison, June 24, 1789, DHFFC, XVI, 849–50, and Veit, 253–54.

6. Jonathan Swift, *A Tale of a Tub* (George Routledge and Sons, 1889), 50; George Mason to John Mason, July 31, 1789, in Edward A. Rutland, ed., *The Papers of George Mason* (University of North Carolina Press, 1970), Vol. 3, 1162–67.

7. John Fenno to Joseph Ward, July 5, 1789, DHFFC, XVI, 947, and Veit, 258–59.

8. For *The Congressional Register*'s coverage of this July 21 debate, see DHFFC, XI, 1158–63, and Veit, 97–103.

9. DHFFC, XI, 1163.

10. For the appointment of the committee, see DHFFC, III, 117.

11. Ibid., 124–25.

12. For Madison's original amendment proposals, see Appendix.

13. For James Otis Jr.'s speech, see Edward Widmer, *American Speeches: Political Oratory from the Revolution to the Civil War* (Library of America, 2006), 1–5. See also John J. Waters Jr., *The Otis Family in Provincial and Revolutionary Massachusetts* (University of North Carolina Press, 1968); Bernard Bailyn, *The Ordeal of Thomas Hutchinson* (Belknap Press of Harvard University Press, 1974), 48, 54–56. For the Quartering Acts of 1765 and 1774, see the Yale University Avalon Project (Avalon.law.yale.edu). See also Gordon S. Wood, *The American Revolution* (Modern Library, 2002), 31–32; Robert S. Middlekauf, *The Glorious Cause* (Oxford University Press, 1982); and Edmund S. Morgan, *The Birth of the Republic, 1763–89*, 4th ed. (University of Chicago Press, 2013), 33–36. For Lexington and Concord, see Robert A. Gross, *The Minutemen and Their World* (Hill and Wang, 2001).

14. For a discussion of religious minorities and religious liberty in the eighteenth century, see, for example, John A. Ragosta, *Wellspring of Liberty: How Virginia's Religious Dissenters Helped Win the American Revolution and Secure Religious Liberty* (Oxford University Press, 2010).

15. See James D. Rice, *Tales from a Revolution: Bacon's Rebellion and the Transformation of Early America* (Oxford University Press, 2013); Edmund S. Morgan, *American Slavery, American Freedom* (Norton, 2003); Wilcomb E. Washburn, *The Governor and the Rebel: A History of Bacon's Rebellion in Virginia* (Norton 1972).

16. See Kevin Kenny, *Peaceable Kingdom Lost: The Paxton Boys and the Destruction of William Penn's Holy Experiment* (Oxford University Press, 2011).

17. See Marjoleine Kars, *Breaking Loose Together: The Regulator Rebellion in Pre-Revolutionary North Carolina* (University of North Carolina Press, 2001); Carole W. Troxler, *Farming Dissenters: The Regulator Movement in Piedmont North Carolina* (North Carolina Office of Archives and History, 2011).

18. See Carol Berkin, *A Brilliant Solution: Inventing the American Constitution* (Harcourt, 2002), 26–29; Richard Beeman, *Plain Honest Men: The Making of the American Constitution* (Random House, reprint, 2010); David P. Szatmary, *Shays' Rebellion: The Making of an Agrarian Insurrection* (University of Massachusetts Press, 1984).

19. See Jill Lepore, *New York Burning: Liberty, Slavery, and Conspiracy in Eighteenth-Century Manhattan* (Vintage, reprint ed., 2006); Peter C. Hoffer, *Cry*

Liberty: The Great Stono River Slave Rebellion of 1739 (Oxford University Press, 2011). See also Craig Steven Wilder, *In the Company of Black Men: The African Influence on African American Culture in New York City* (New York University Press, 2001), 16–17.

Chapter Eight

1. DHFFC, III, 130.

2. John Brown to Harry Innes, August 3, 1789, DHFFC, XVI, 1223–24; Roger Sherman to Henry Gibbs, August 4, 1789, DHFFC, XVI, 1237, and Veit, 271.

3. See DHFFC, III, 130–33. For the record of the debates from August 13 until August 26, see DHFFC, III, 148–70, and DHFFC, XI, 1207–1329. These debates are also reproduced in Veit, 104–213.

4. DHFFC, XI, 1218.

5. DHFFC, XI, 1213, and Veit, 109.

6. DHFFC, XI, 1228, and Veit, 124.

7. "Pacificus" to James Madison, August 14, 1789, *New York Daily Advertiser,* in Veit, 275–77; for the identification of Noah Webster as "Pacificus," see Kenneth R. Bowling, " 'A Tub to the Whale': The Founding Fathers and the Adoption of the Federal Bill of Rights," *Journal of the Early Republic,* Vol. 8, No. 3 (Autumn 1988), 225. See also James Madison to Edmund Pendleton, August 21, 1789, and James Madison to Edmund Randolph, August 21, 1789, in Robert A. Rutland et al., eds., *The Papers of James Madison* (University Press of Virginia, 1977), Vol. 12, 348–49, and Veit, 284.

8. DHFFC, XI, 1262; Veit, 158–59.

9. For a discussion of Madison's concern about state legislatures and abuse of power, see Gordon Wood, "Interests and Disinterestedness in the Making of the Constituton," in Richard Beeman, Stephen Botein, and Edward C. Carter, eds., *Beyond Confederation: Origins of the Constitution and American National Identity* (University of North Carolina Press, 1987), 69–109.

10. DHFFC, XI, 1265; Veit, 154.

11. DHFFC, XI, 1266–67; Veit, 163.

12. DHFFC, XI, 1268–70; Veit, 155, 166.

13. DHFFC, XI, 1271–72; (Madison), 1272–74 (Gerry).

14. Ibid., 1274.

15. Ibid., 1275; Veit, 171.

16. DHFFC, XI, 1276.

17. Ibid., 1281; Veit, 177–78.

18. DHFFC, XI, 1281.

19. William Smith to Edward Rutledge, August 15, 1789, DHFFC, XVI, 1327.

Chapter Nine

1. John Brown to William Irvine, August 17, 1789, DHFFC, XVI, 1336–37.

2. For the debate on "well regulated militia," see DHFFC, XI, 1285–89.

3. On the prohibition on quartering troops, Roger Sherman demurred. He believed quartering was a practical necessity when the troops were militiamen. See Scott D. Gerber, "Roger Sherman and the Bill of Rights," *Polity*, Vol. 28, No. 4 (Summer 1996), 521–40.

4. DHFFC, XI, 1290–92.

5. Ibid., 1290–91.

6. Ibid., 1292.

7. Veit, 190.

8. Ibid., 191.

9. For Tucker's remarks, see DHFFC, XI, 1297–99, and Veit, 194–95.

10. DHFFC, XI, 1300; Veit, 197.

11. DHFFC, XI, 1301; Veit, 197.

12. For the debates in the House on the report of the committee of the whole, August 18–22, and the proposed changes and amendments to the committee version, see DHFFC, III, 151–65.

13. William Smith to Otho Holland Williams, DHFFC, XVI, 1337–38; Frederick

Muhlenberg to Benjamin Rush, August 18, 1789, DHFFC, XVI, 1347–49, and Veit, 280–81.

14. James Madison to Richard Peters, August 19, 1789, DHFFC, XVI, 1354–55, and Veit, 282.

Chapter Ten

1. George Clymer to Benjamin Rush, August 17, 1789, DHFFC, XVI, 1344.

2. DHFFC, XI, 1308; Veit, 198.

3. Veit, 198.

4. James Madison to Richard Peters, DHFFC, XVI, 1354–56.

5. DHFFC, XI, 1308–09; Veit, 198.

6. DHFFC, XI, 1310, and, for the full day's debate and discussion, 1309–16.

7. Ibid., 1310.

8. Ibid., 1311–12.

9. Ibid., 1313–14; Benjamin Goodhue to Michael Hodge, August 20, 1789, DHFFC, XVI, 1359.

10. See John C. Meleney, *The Public Life of Aedanus Burke: Revolutionary Republican in Post-Revolutionary South Carolina* (University of South Carolina Press,1989).

11. DHFFC, XI, 1314–15.

12. Ibid.: for the *Gazette*'s account, 1316–18; for the *Congressional Register*'s fuller coverage of this debate, 1319–24.

13. DHFFC, XI, 1321–22.

Chapter Eleven

1. Benjamin Goodhue to Insurance Offices of Salem, August 23, 1789, DHFFC, XVI, 1379; William Smith to Otho H. Williams, August 22, 1789, DHFFC, XVI, 1376*n*. For a discussion of dueling and honor in the early republic, see Joanne Freeman, *Affairs of Honor: National Politics in the New Republic* (Yale University Press, 2002).

2. Benjamin Goodhue to Insurance Offices of Salem, August 23, 1789, DHFFC, XVI, 1379.

3. Robert Morris to Richard Peters, August 24, 1789, DHFFC, XVI, 1391–93.

4. For brief biographical sketches of the senators, see back matter.

5. William Maclay, *Journal of William Maclay, United States Senator from Pennsylvania* (Forgotten Books, 2012), August 26, 1789, 138.

6. Ibid., 134; see also Veit, 289.

7. Maclay, *Journal,* 144–56.

8. For the senate version of the amendments see Veit, 47–49.

9. Benjamin Goodhue to Samuel Phillips, September 13, 1789, DHFFC, XVII, 1528, and Veit, 294. See also Benjamin Goodhue to Michael Hodge, September 20, 1789, DHFFC, XVII, 1585.

10. Theodorick Bland Randolph to St. George Tucker, September 9, 1789, DHFFC, XVII, 1507.

11. Ibid.; John Randolph to St. George Tucker, September 11, 1789, DHFFC, XVII, 1510, and Veit, 293.

12. Richard Henry Lee to Francis Lightfoot Lee, September 13, 1789, DHFFC, XVII, 1532, and Veit, 294.

13. Elbridge Gerry to John Wendell, September 14, 1789, DHFFC, XVII, 1540, and Veit, 294.

14. Richard Henry Lee to Patrick Henry, September 14, 1789, DHFFC, XVII, 1542, and Veit 296.

15. James Madison to Edmund Pendleton, September 14, 1789, DHFFC, XVII, 1544.

16. Fisher Ames to Caleb Strong, September 15, 1789, ibid., 1550, and Veit, 297.

17. Paine Wingate to John Langdon, September 17, 1789, DHFFC, XVII, 1570, and Veit, 297.

18. Richard Henry Lee to Patrick Henry, September 27, 1789, DHFFC, XVII, 1625, and Veit, 298–99.

19. William Grayson to Patrick Henry, September 29, 1789, DHFFC, XVII, 1641, and Veit, 300; Richard Henry Lee and William Grayson to Thomas Mathews, speaker of the Virginia house of delegates, September 28, 1789, DHFFC, XVII, 1634.

20. Thomas Tudor Tucker to St. George Tucker, October 2, 1789, DHFFC, XVII, 1657.

Chapter Twelve

1. *Providence* (Rhode Island) *Gazette,* October 3, 1789, and *Salem* (Massachusetts) *Mercury,* October 13, 1789, DHFFC, XVII, 1652, 1679.

2. Elbridge Gerry to Ann Gerry, November 22, 1789, ibid., 1717.

3. Ibid.: Fisher Ames to Theodore Sedgwick, October 6, 1789, 1671–73; William Smith to Edward Rutledge, October 6, 1789, 1673–74; William Grayson to James Madison, October 7, 1789, 1675–77. See also Richard Labunski, *James Madison and the Struggle for the Bill of Rights,* (Oxford University Press, 2006), 244.

4. Comte de Moustier to Comte de Montmorin, October 3, 1789, DHFFC, XVII, 1658–65.

5. For a discussion of the state ratification debates and decisions, see Joseph Gales, *The Debates and Proceedings in the Congress of the United States: With an Appendix, Containing Important State Papers and Public Documents* (Gales and Seaton, 1834), Vol. 2, 2034–40. See also DHFFC, III, 577–97; Kenneth R. Bowling, "Overshadowed by States' Rights: Ratification of the Federal Bill of Rights," in Ronald Hoffman and Peter J. Albert, eds., *The Bill of Rights: Government Proscribed* (University Press of Virginia, 1997), 77–102; Kenneth R. Bowling, " 'A Tub to the Whale': The Founding Fathers and Adoption of the Federal Bill of Rights," *Journal of the Early Republic,* Vol. 8, No. 3 (Autumn 1988), 248–50; John Kaminski, "The Making of the Bill of Rights 1787–1792," in Stephen L. Schechter and Richard B. Bernstein, *Contexts of the Bill of Rights* (New York State Commission on the Bicentennial of the United States Constitution, 1990), 18–64; Leonard W. Levy, "Why We Have the Bill of Rights," in *Origins of the Bill of Rights* (Yale University Press, 1999), 40–43; Labunski, *James Madison,* 245–55.

6. See Bowling, "Overshadowed by States' Rights," 85–86.

7. See Kaminski, "The Making of the Bill of Rights," 51–54; Bowling, "Overshadowed by States' Rights," 86–87.

8. See Kaminski, "The Making of the Bill of Rights, 87–88; Bowling, "Overshadowed by States' Rights," 87–88.

9. The Centinel, XXIX (Samuel Bryan), *Independent Gazetteer,* September 9, 1789.

10. Richard Henry Lee and William Grayson to Thomas Matthews, Speaker of the Virginia House of Delegates, September 28, 1789, and Richard Henry Lee and William Grayson to Governor Beverley Randolph, September 28, 1789, DHFFC, XVII, 1634–35.

11. For the Report on Public Credit, see Harold C. Syrett, ed., *The Papers of Alexander Hamilton* (Columbia University Press, 1961) Vol. 6, 67–72; Henry Lee to James Madison, April 3, 1790, James Madison Papers, LC, Series 1, General Correspondence and Related Items, 1723–1859.

12. Hamilton submitted his Second Report on Public Credit to Congress, calling for a national bank, on December 13, 1790. See American State Papers, House of Representatives, 1st Congress, 3rd Session, Finance, Vol. 1, LC.

13. Richard Brookhiser, *Alexander Hamilton, American* (Simon and Schuster, 2000), 82. For a full discussion of the Virginia ratification process, see J. Gordon Hylton, "Virginia and the Ratification of the Bill of Rights, 1789–1791," *University of Richmond Law Review,* Vol. 25 (1991), 433.

Epilogue

1. See Pauline Maier, *American Scripture: Making the Declaration of Independence* (Vintage, 1998), chap. 4 and Epilogue, 154–216.

2. See William Watkins, *Reclaiming the American Revolution: The Kentucky and Virginia Resolutions and Their Legacy* (Palgrave Macmillan, 2008); Forrest McDonald, *States' Rights and the Union: Imperium in Imperio, 1776–1876* (University Press of Kansas, reprint ed., 2002).

Biographies of Members of the First Federal Congress

Members of the Senate

1. A note on terminology: The Confederation Congress called itself the Continental Congress. In addition, some delegates defy easy categorization as Federalist or

Antifederalist, as they voted for ratification but took antiadministration positions during their term in Congress and they are thus classified differently by historians.

2. Eben F. Stone, "A Sketch of Tristram Dalton," in *Historical Collections of the Essex Institute,* Vol. 25, (January, February, March 1888), nos. 1, 2, 3, 1–29.

3. Cyrus Mason Tracy, *Standard History of Essex County, Massachusetts, Embracing a History of the County from Its First Settlement to the Present Time: With a History and Description of Its Towns and Cities* (C. F. Jewett and Company, 1878), 420; George Drew Merrill, *History of Coos County, New Hampshire* (W. A. Fergusson and Company, 1888), 506.

4. Stone, "A Sketch of Tristram Dalton," 29.

5. William Pierce, "Notes of Major William Pierce on the Federal Convention of 1787," *American Historical Review,* Vol. 3, No. 2 (January 1898), 326–27.

6. James V. Marshall, *The United States Manual of Biography and History* (James B. Smith and Company, 1856), 188.

7. Weston Bristow, "William Grayson: A Study in Virginia Biography of the Eighteenth Century," *Richmond College Historical Papers* (June 1917), 74–117.

8. George R. Lamplugh, "The Importance of Being Truculent: James Gunn, the Chatham Militia, and Georgia Politics, 1782–1789," *Georgia Historical Quarterly,* Vol. 80, No. 2 (Summer 1996), 227–45.

9. *The Letters of Pierce Butler, 1790–1794: Nation Building and Enterprise in the New American Republic* (University of South Carolina Press, 2007), 113–14.

10. J. Winfield Henry, ed., *Letters and Papers of Governor John Henry of Maryland* (George W. King Printing Company, 1904), 77.

11. Anne Izard Deas, ed., to *Correspondence of Mr. Ralph Izard of South Carolina from the Year 1774 to 1804 with a Short Memoir* (C. S. Francis, 1844), Vol. 1; Langdon Cheves, "Izard of South Carolina," *South Carolina Historical and Genealogical Magazine* (Walker, Evans, and Cogswell Company, 1900), Vol. 2, 208.

12. Herbert Storing, *What the Antifederalists Were For: The Political Thought of the Opponents of the Constitution* (University of Chicago Press, 1981), 17.

13. William Graham Sumner, *Robert Morris* (Dodd, Mead, 1892), 127, 162.

14. Pierce, "Notes of Major William Pierce on the Federal Convention of 1787," 328.

Members of the House of Representatives

1. Benjamin Goodhue to Samuel Phillips, August 11, 1789, DHFFC, XVI, 1290, 1291.

2. Margaret C. S. Christman, "Unraveling a Mistaken Identity Profile," *Smithsonian National Portrait Gallery News*, Vol. 1, No. 3 (Fall 2000), 10.

3. Speech to the Faculty and Students of the York Academy of York, *Pennsylvania Herald*, February 23, 1789.

4. Richard W. Hull, "John Hathorn, Warwick's Forgotten Patriot," *Warwick Valley Dispatch*, August 4, 2004.

5. *The Huntington Letters: In the Possession of Julia Chester Wells*, Appleton Press, 1897, BH to Anne H, September 8, 1783, pp. 56–61.

6. George R. Lamplugh, "Oh the Colossus! The Colossus! James Jackson and the Jeffersonian Republican Party in Georgia, 1796–1806," *Journal of the Early Republic*, Vol. 9, No. 3 (Autumn 1989), 315–34.

7. Tom Hester, "Queens Rangers Raid Brings Destruction and Horror," *Star-Ledger* (New Jersey), Part 15, October 29, 1779.

8. *Historical Magazine of Monongahela's Old Home Coming Week*, September 6–13, 1908, in Historic Pittsburgh General Text Collection, 50.

9. Albert Matthews, ed., "Journal of William Loughton Smith, 1790–1791," *Proceedings of the Massachusetts Historical Society* (October 1917), 25.

10. George Folsom, *History of Saco and Biddeford: With Notices of Other Early Settlements, and of Proprietary Governments, in Maine, Including the Provinces of New Somersetshire and Lygonia* (A. C. Putnam, 1830), 302.

11. Diana Dru Dowdy, " 'A School for Stoicism': Thomas Tudor Tucker and the Republican Age," *South Carolina Historical Magazine*, Vol. 96, No. 2 (April 1995), 102–18.

12. A. Douglas Proctor, "Colonel Jeremiah Wadsworth," *Connecticut Society of the Sons of the American Revolution Newsletter*, 1999.

Index